Pauline Kael on the best film ever made

Raising Kane

Pauline Kael

First published in *The New Yorker* copyright © 1971

First published as Raising Kane in *The New Yorker*
Copyright © 1971 Pauline Kael

First published in 1971 by Martin Secker & Warburg Ltd
Published in 1985 by Methuen London Ltd
Reprinted in 1989 by Methuen Drama

Reprinted in 2002 by Methuen Publishing Ltd
215 Vauxhall Bridge Road, London, SW1V 1EJ

This edition is exclusive to *Sight and Sound* magazine
by arrangement with Methuen Publishing Ltd.
Sight and Sound is published monthly by the British Film Institute.

Printed and bound in Great Britain
by Cox and Wyman Ltd, Reading, Berkshire

Raising Kane

Pauline Kael

without the contours of his particular villainy – they neverthe-less respond to the effrontery, the audacity, and the risks. Hearst's career and his power provided a dangerous subject that stimulated and energized all those connected with the picture – they felt they were *doing* something instead of just working on one more cooked-up story that didn't relate to anything that mattered. And to the particular kinds of people who shaped this enterprise the dangers involved made the subject irresistible.

Citizen Kane, the film that, as Truffaut said, is 'probably the one that has started the largest number of filmmakers on their careers,' was not an ordinary assignment. It is one of the few films ever made inside a major studio in the United States *in freedom* – not merely in freedom from interference but in freedom from the routine methods of experienced directors. George J. Schaefer, who, with the help of Nelson Rockefeller, had become president of R.K.O. late in 1938, when it was struggling to avert bankruptcy, needed a miracle to save the company, and after the national uproar over Orson Welles' *The War of the Worlds* broadcast Rockefeller apparently thought that Welles – 'the wonder boy' – might come up with one, and urged Schaefer to get him. But Welles, who was committed to the theatre and wasn't especially enthusiastic about making movies, rejected the first offers; he held out until Schaefer offered him complete control over his productions. Then Welles brought out to Hollywood from New York his own production unit – the Mercury Theatre company, a group of actors and associates he could count on – and, because he was inexperienced in movies and was smart and had freedom, he was able to find in Hollywood people who had been waiting all their lives to try out new ideas. So a miracle did come about, though it was not the kind of miracle R.K.O. needed.

Kane does something so well, and with such spirit, that the fullness and completeness of it continue to satisfy us. The

4

formal elements themselves produce elation; we are kept aware of how marvellously worked out the ideas are. It would be high-toned to call this method of keeping the audience aware 'Brechtian,' and it would be wrong. It comes out of a different tradition – the same commercial-comedy tradition that Walter Kerr analyzed so beautifully in his review of the 1969 Broadway revival of *The Front Page*, the 1928 play by Ben Hecht and Charles MacArthur, when he said, 'A play was held to be something of a machine in those days. ... It was a machine for surprising and delighting the audience, regularly, logically, insanely, but accountably. A play was like a watch that laughed.' The mechanics of movies are rarely as entertaining as they are in *Citizen Kane*, as cleverly designed to be the kind of fun that keeps one alert and conscious of the enjoyment of the artifices themselves.

Walter Kerr goes on to describe the second-act entrance prepared for Walter Burns, the scheming, ruthless managing editor of *The Front Page*:

> He can't just come on and declare himself. ... He's got to walk into a tough situation in order to be brutally noncha-lant, which is what we think is funny about him. The machinery has not only given him and the play the right punctuation, the change of pace that refreshes even as it moves on. It has also covered him, kept him from being obvious while exploiting the one most obvious thing about him. You might say that the machinery has covered itself, perfectly squared itself. We are delighted to have the man on, we are delighted to have him on at this time, we are aware that it is sleight-of-hand that has got him on, and we are as delighted by the sleight-of-hand as by the man.

Citizen Kane is made up of an astonishing number of such bits of technique, and of sequences built to make their points and get their laughs and hit climax just before a fast cut takes us to the next. It is practically a collection of blackout sketches, but blackout sketches arranged to comment on each other, and it was planned that way right in the shooting script.

It is difficult to explain what makes any great work great, and particularly difficult with movies, and maybe more so with *Citizen Kane* than with other great movies, because it isn't a work of special depth or a work of subtle beauty. It is a shallow work, a *shallow* masterpiece. Those who try to account for its stature as a film by claiming it to be profound are simply dodging the problem – or maybe they don't recognize that there is one. Like most of the films of the sound era that are called masterpieces, *Citizen Kane* has reached its audience gradually over the years rather than at the time of release. Yet, unlike the others, it is conceived and acted as entertainment in a popular style (unlike, say, *Rules of the Game* or *Rashomon* or *Man of Aran*, which one does not think of in crowd-pleasing terms). Apparently, the easiest thing for people to do when they recognize that something is a work of art is to trot out the proper schoolbook terms for works of art, and there are articles on *Citizen Kane* that call it a tragedy in fugal form and articles that explain that the hero of *Citizen Kane* is time – time being a proper sort of modern hero for an important picture. But to use the conventional schoolbook explanations for greatness, and pretend that it's profound, is to miss what makes it such an American triumph – that it manages to create something aesthetically exciting and durable out of the playfulness of American muckraking satire. *Kane* is closer to comedy than to tragedy, though so overwrought in style as to be almost a Gothic comedy. What might possibly be considered tragic in it has such a Daddy Warbucks quality that if it's tragic at all it's comic-strip tragic. The mystery in *Kane* is largely fake, and the Gothic-thriller atmosphere and the Rosebud gimmickry (though fun) are such obvious penny-dreadful popular theatrics that they're not so very different from the fake mysteries that Hearst's *American Weekly* used to whip up – the haunted castles and the curses fulfilled. *Citizen Kane* is a 'popular' masterpiece – not in terms of actual popularity but in terms of its conceptions and the way it gets its laughs and makes its points. Possibly it was too complexly told to be one of the greatest commercial successes, but we can't really tell whether it might have become even a modest success, because it didn't get a fair chance.

2

Orson Welles brought forth a miracle, but he couldn't get by with it. Though Hearst made some direct attempts to interfere with the film, it wasn't so much what he did that hurt the film commercially as what others feared he might do, to them and to the movie industry. They knew he was contemplating action, so they did the picture in for him; it was as if they decided whom the king might want killed, and, eager to oblige, performed the murder without waiting to be asked. Before *Kane* opened, George J. Schaefer was summoned to New York by Nicholas Schenck, the chairman of the board of Loew's International, the M-G-M affiliate that controlled the distribution of M-G-M pictures. Schaefer had staked just about everything on Welles, and the picture looked like a winner, but now Schenk made Schaefer a cash offer from Louis B. Mayer, the head of production at M-G-M, of $842,000 if Schaefer would destroy the negative and all the prints. The picture had actually cost only $686,033; the offer handsomely included a fair amount for the post-production costs.

Mayer's motive may have been partly friendship and loyalty to Hearst, even though Hearst, who had formerly been associated with M-G-M, had, some years earlier, after a dispute with Irving Thalberg, taken his investment out of

M-G-M and moved his star, Marion Davies, and his money to Warner Brothers. M-G-M had lost money on a string of costume clinkers starring Miss Davies (*Beverly of Graustark*, et al.), and had even lost money on some of her good pictures, but Mayer had got free publicity for M-G-M releases out of the connection with Hearst, and had also got what might be called deep personal satisfaction. In 1929, when Herbert Hoover invited the Mayers to the White House – they were the first 'informal' guests after his inauguration – Hearst's *New York American* gave the visit a full column. Mayer enjoyed fraternizing with Hearst and his eminent guests; photographs show Mayer with Hearst and Lindbergh, Mayer with Hearst and Winston Churchill, Mayer at lunch with Bernard Shaw and Marion Davies – but they never, of course, show Mayer with both Hearst and Miss Davies. Candid cameramen sometimes caught the two together, but Hearst, presumably out of respect for his wife, did not pose in groups that included Miss Davies. Despite the publicity showered on her in the Hearst papers, the forms were carefully observed. She quietly packed and left for her own house on the rare occasions when Mrs Hearst, who lived in the East, was expected to be in residence at San Simeon. Kane's infatuation for the singer Susan Alexander in the movie was thus a public flaunting of matters that Hearst was careful and considerate about. Because of this, Mayer's longtime friendship for Hearst was probably a lesser factor than the fear that the Hearst press would reveal some sordid stories about the movie moguls and join in one of those recurrent crusades against movie immorality, like the one that had destroyed Fatty Arbuckle's career. The movie industry was frightened of reprisals. (The movie industry is always frightened, and is always proudest of films that celebrate courage.) As one of the trade papers phrased it in those nervous weeks when no one knew whether the picture would be released, 'the industry could ill afford to be made the object of counterattack by the Hearst newspapers.'

There were rumors that Hearst was mounting a general campaign; his legal staff had seen the script, and Louella Parsons, the Hearst movie columnist, who had attended a screening of the film flanked by lawyers, was agitated and had swung into action. The whole industry, it was feared, would take the rap for R.K.O.'s indiscretion, and, according to the trade press at the time (and Schaefer confirms this report), Mayer was not putting up the $842,000 all by himself. It was a joint offer from the top movie magnates, who were combining for common protection. The offer was presented to Schaefer on the ground that it was in the best interests of everybody concerned – which was considered to be the entire, threatened industry – for *Citizen Kane* to be destroyed. Rather astonishingly, Schaefer refused. He didn't confer with his board of directors, because, he says, he had good reason to think they would tell him to accept. He refused even though R.K.O., having few theatres of its own, was dependent on the other companies and he had been warned that the big theatre circuits – controlled by the men who wanted the picture destroyed – would refuse to show it.

Schaefer knew the spot he was in. The première had been tentatively set for February 14th at the Radio City Music Hall – usually the showcase for big R.K.O. pictures, because R.K.O. was partly owned by the Rockefellers and the Chase National Bank, who owned the Music Hall. The manager of the theatre had been enthusiastic about the picture. Then, suddenly, the Music Hall turned it down. Schaefer phoned Nelson Rockefeller to find out why, and, he says, 'Rockefeller told me that Louella Parsons had warned him off it, that she had asked him, "How would you like to have the *American Weekly* magazine section run a double-page spread on John D. Rockefeller?"' According to Schaefer, she also called David Sarnoff, another large investor in R.K.O., and similarly threatened him. In mid-February, with a minor contract dispute serving as pretext, the Hearst papers blasted R.K.O. and Schaefer in front-page stories; it was an unmistakable public warning. Schaefer was stranded; he had to scrounge for theatres, and, amid the general fear that Hearst might sue and would almost certainly remove advertising for any houses that showed *Citizen Kane*, he couldn't get bookings. The solution was for R.K.O. to take the risks of any lawsuits, but when the company leased an independent theatre in Los Angeles and refurbished the Palace (then a vaudeville house), which R.K.O. owned, for the New York opening, and did the same for a theatre R.K.O. owned in Chicago, Schaefer had trouble launching an advertising campaign. (Schenck, not surprisingly, owned a piece of the biggest movie-advertising agency.) Even after the early rave reviews and the initial enthusiasm, Schaefer couldn't get bookings except in the theatres that R.K.O. itself owned and in a few small art houses that were willing to take the risk. Eventually, in order to get the picture into theatres, Schaefer threatened to sue Warners', Fox, Paramount, and Loew's on a charge of conspiracy. (There was reason to believe the company heads had promised Hearst they wouldn't show it in their theatres.) Warners' (perhaps afraid of exposure and the troubles with their stockholders that might result from a lawsuit) gave in and booked the picture, and the others followed, halfheartedly – in some cases, theatres paid for the picture but didn't play it.

By then, just about everybody in the industry was scared, or mad, or tired of the whole thing, and though the feared general reprisals against the industry did not take place, R.K.O. was getting bruised. The Hearst papers banned publicity on R.K.O. pictures and dropped an announced serialization of the novel *Kitty Foyle* which had been timed for the release of the R.K.O. film version. Some R.K.O. films didn't get reviewed and others got bad publicity. It was all petty harassment, of a kind that could be blamed on the overzealous Miss Parsons and other Hearst employees, but it was obviously sanctioned by Hearst, and it was steady enough to keep the industry uneasy.

By the time *Citizen Kane* got into Warners' theatres, the picture had acquired such an odd reputation that people seemed to distrust it, and it didn't do very well. It was subsequently withdrawn from circulation, perhaps because of the vicissitudes of R.K.O., and until the late fifties, when it was reissued and began to play in the art houses and to attract a new audience, it was seen only in pirated versions in 16 mm. Even after Mayer had succeeded in destroying the picture commercially, he went on planning vengeance on Schaefer for refusing his offer. Stockholders in R.K.O. began to hear that the company wasn't prospering because Schaefer was anti-Semitic and was therefore having trouble getting proper distribution for R.K.O. pictures. Schaefer says that Mayer wanted to get control of R.K.O. and that the rumor was created to drive down the price of the stock – that Mayer hoped to scare out Floyd Odlum, a major stockholder, and buy his shares. Instead, Odlum, who had opposed Nelson Rockefeller's choice of Schaefer to run the company, bought enough of Sarnoff's stock to have a controlling interest, and by mid-1942 Schaefer was finished at R.K.O. Two weeks after he left, Welles' unit was evicted from its offices on the lot and given a few hours to move out, and the R.K.O. employees who had worked with Welles were punished with degrading assignments on B pictures. Mayer's friendship with Hearst was not ruffled. A few years later, when Mayer left his wife of forty years, he rented Marion Davies' Beverly Hills mansion. Eventually, he was one of Hearst's honorary pallbearers. *Citizen Kane* didn't actually lose money, but in Hollywood bookkeeping it wasn't a big enough moneymaker to balance the scandal.

3

Welles was recently quoted as saying, 'Theatre is a collective experience; cinema is the work of one single person.' This is an extraordinary remark from the man who brought his own Mercury Theatre players to Hollywood (fifteen of them appeared in *Citizen Kane*), and also the Mercury co-producer John Houseman, the Mercury composer Bernard Herrmann, and various assistants, such as Richard Wilson, William Alland, and Richard Barr. He not only brought his whole supportive group – his family, he called them then – but found people in Hollywood, such as the cinematographer Gregg Toland, to contribute their knowledge and gifts to *Citizen Kane*. Orson Welles has done some marvellous things in his later movies – some great things – and there is more depth in the somewhat botched *The Magnificent Ambersons*, of 1942 (which also used many of the Mercury players), than in *Citizen Kane*, but his principal career in the movies has been in adaptation, as it was earlier on the stage. He has never again worked on a subject with the immediacy and impact of *Kane*. His later films – even those he has so painfully struggled to finance out of his earnings as an actor – haven't been *conceived* in terms of daring modern subjects that excite us, as the very idea of *Kane* excited us. This particular kind of journalist's sense of what would be a scandal as well as a great subject, and the ability to write it, belonged not to Welles but to his now almost forgotten associate Herman J. Mankiewicz, who wrote the script, and who inadvertently destroyed the picture's chances. There is a theme that is submerged in much of *Citizen Kane* but that comes to the surface now and then, and it's the linking life story of Hearst and of Mankiewicz and of Welles – the story of how brilliantly gifted men who seem to have everything it takes to do what they want to do are defeated. It's the story of how heroes become comedians and con artists.

The Hearst papers ignored Welles – Hearst may have considered this a fit punishment for an actor – though they attacked him indirectly with sneak attacks on those associated with him, and Hearst would frequently activate his secular arm, the American Legion, against him. But the Hearst papers worked Mankiewicz over in headlines; they persecuted him so long that he finally appealed to the American Civil Liberties Union for help. There was some primitive justice in this. Hearst had never met Welles, and, besides, Welles was a kid, a twenty-five-year-old prodigy (whose daughter Marion Davies' nephew was bringing up) – hardly the sort of person one held responsible. But Mankiewicz was a friend of both Marion Davies and Hearst, and had been a frequent guest at her beach house and at San Simeon. There, in the great baronial banquet hall, Hearst liked to seat Mankiewicz on his left, so that Mankiewicz, with all his worldliness and wit (the Central Park West Voltaire, Ben Hecht had called him a few years earlier), could entertain the guest of honor and Hearst wouldn't miss any of it. Mankiewicz betrayed their hospitality, even though he liked them both. They must have presented an irresistible target. And so Hearst, the yellow-press lord who had trained Mankiewicz's generation of reporters to betray *anyone* for a story, became at last the victim of his own style of journalism.

4

In the first Academy Award ceremony, for 1927–28, Warner Brothers, which had just produced *The Jazz Singer*, was honored for 'Marking on Epoch in Motion Picture History.' If the first decade of talkies – roughly, the thirties – has never been rivalled in wit and exuberance, this is very largely because there was already in Hollywood in the late silent period a nucleus of the best American writers, and they either lured their friends West or were joined by them. Unlike the novelists who were drawn to Hollywood later, most of the best Hollywood writers of the thirties had a shared background; they had been reporters and critics, and they knew each other from their early days on newspapers and magazines.

In his autobiography, Ben Hecht tells of being broke in New York – it was probably the winter of 1926 – and of getting a telegram from Herman Mankiewicz in Hollywood:

WILL YOU ACCEPT THREE HUNDRED PER WEEK TO WORK FOR PARAMOUNT PICTURES? ALL EXPENSES PAID. THE THREE HUNDRED IS PEANUTS. MILLIONS ARE TO BE GRABBED OUT HERE AND YOUR ONLY COMPETITION IS IDIOTS. DON'T LET THIS GET AROUND.

A newspaper photograph shows Mankiewicz greeting Hecht, 'noted author, dramatist, and former newspaperman,' upon his arrival. After Hecht had begun work at Paramount, he discovered that the studio chief, B. P. Schulberg – who at that time considered writers a waste of money – had been persuaded to hire him by a gambler's ploy: Mankiewicz had offered to tear up his own two-year contract if Hecht failed to write a successful movie. Hecht, that phenomenal fast hack who was to become one of the most prolific of all motion-picture writers (and one of the most frivolously cynical about the results), worked for a week and turned out the script that became Josef von Sternberg's great hit *Underworld*. That script brought Hecht the first Academy Award for an original story, and a few years later he initiated the practice of using Oscars as doorstops. The studio heads knew what they had in Hecht as soon as they read the script, and they showed their gratitude. Hecht has recorded:

I was given a ten-thousand-dollar check as a bonus for the

week's work, a check which my sponsor Mankiewicz snatched out of my hand as I was bowing my thanks.

'You'll have it back in a week,' Manky said. 'I just want it for a few days to get me out of a little hole.'

He gambled valiantly, tossing a coin in the air with Eddie Cantor and calling heads or tails for a thousand dollars. He lost constantly. He tried to get himself secretly insured behind his good wife Sara's back, planning to hock the policy and thus meet his obligation. This plan collapsed when the insurance-company doctor refused to accept him as a risk.

I finally solved the situation by taking Manky into the Front Office and informing the studio bosses of our joint dilemma. I asked that my talented friend be given a five-hundred-a-week raise. The studio could then deduct this raise from his salary. . . .

I left . . . with another full bonus check in my hand; and Manky, with his new raise, became the highest paid writer for Paramount Pictures, Inc.

The bait that brought the writers in was money, but those writers who, like Mankiewicz, helped set the traps had their own reason: conviviality. Mankiewicz's small joke 'Don't let this get around' came from a man who lived for talk, a man who saw moviemaking as too crazy, too profitable, and too *easy* not to share with one's friends. By the early thirties, the writers who lived in Hollywood or commuted there included not only Mankiewicz and Hecht and Charles MacArthur but George S. Kaufman and Marc Connelly, and Nathanael West and his brother-in-law S. J. Perelman, and Preston Sturges, Dorothy Parker, Arthur Kober, Alice Duer Miller, John O'Hara, Donald Ogden Stewart, Samson Raphaelson (the *New York Times* reporter who wrote the play *The Jazz Singer*), Gene Fowler, and Nunnally Johnson, and such already famous

15

playwrights as Philip Barry, S. N. Behrman, Maxwell Anderson, Robert E. Sherwood, and Sidney Howard. Scott Fitzgerald had already been there for his first stretch, in 1927, along with Edwin Justus Mayer, and by 1932 William Faulkner began coming and going, and from time to time Ring Lardner and Moss Hart would turn up. In earlier periods, American writers made a living on newspapers and magazines; in the forties and fifties, they went into the academies (or, once they got to college, never left). But in the late twenties and the thirties they went to Hollywood. And though, apparently, they one and all experienced it as prostitution of their talents – joyous prostitution in some cases – and though more than one fell in love with movies and thus suffered not only from personal frustration but from the corruption of the great, still new art, they nonetheless as a group were responsible for that sustained feat of careless magic we call 'thirties comedy.' *Citizen Kane* was, I think, its culmination.

5

Herman J. Mankiewicz, born in New York City in 1897, was the first son of a professor of education, and then took a teaching position in Wilkes-Barre, where his second son, Joseph L. Mankiewicz, was born in 1909, and where the boys and a sister grew up. Herman Mankiewicz graduated from Columbia in 1916, and after a period as managing editor of the *American Jewish Chronicle* he became a flying cadet with the United States Army in 1917 and, in 1918, a private first class with the Fifth Marines, 2nd Division, A.E.F. In 1919 and 1920, he was the director of the American Red Cross News Service in Paris, and after returning to this country to marry a great beauty, Miss Sara Aaronson, of Baltimore, he took his bride overseas with him while he worked as a foreign correspondent in Berlin from 1920 to 1922, doing political reporting for George Seldes on the *Chicago Tribune*. During that time, he also sent pieces on drama and books to the *New York Times* and *Women's Wear*. Hired in Berlin by Isadora Duncan, he became her publicity man for her return to America. At home again, he took a job as a reporter for the *New York World*. He was a gifted, prodigious writer, who contributed to *Vanity Fair*, the *Saturday Evening Post*, and many other magazines, and, while still in his twenties, collaborated with Heywood Broun, Dorothy Parker, Robert E. Sherwood, and others on a revue (*Round the Town*), and collaborated with George S. Kaufman on a play (*The Good Fellow*) and with Marc Connelly on another play (*The Wild Man of Borneo*). From 1923 to 1926, he was at the *Times*, backing up George S. Kaufman in the drama department; while he was there, he also became the first regular theatre critic for *The New Yorker*, writing weekly from June, 1925, until January, 1926, when Walter Wanger offered him a motion-picture contract and he left for Hollywood. The first picture he wrote was the Lon Chaney success *The Road to Mandalay*. In all, he worked on over seventy movies. He went on living and working in Los Angeles until his death, in 1953. He left three children: Don, born in Berlin in 1922, who is a novelist (*Trial*) and a writer for the movies (co-scenarist of *I Want to Live!*) and television ('Marcus Welby, M.D.'); Frank, born in New York in 1924, who became a lawyer, a journalist, a Peace Corps worker, and Robert Kennedy's press assistant, and is now a columnist and television commentator; and Johanna, born in Los Angeles in 1937, who is a journalist (on *Time*) and is married to Peter Davis, the writer-producer of 'The Selling of the Pentagon.'

Told this way, Herman Mankiewicz's career sounds exemplary, but these are just the bare bones of the truth. Even though it would be easy to document this official life of the apparently rising young man with photographs of Mankiewicz in his Berlin days dining with the Chancellor, Mankiewicz in his newspaperman days outside the *Chicago Tribune* with Jack

Dempsey, and so on, it would be hard to explain his sudden, early aging and the thickening of his features and the transparently cynical look on his face in later photographs.

It was a lucky thing for Mankiewicz that he got the movie job when he did, because he would never have risen at the *Times*, and though he wrote regularly for *The New Yorker* (and remarked of those of the Algonquin group who didn't, 'The part-time help of wits is no better than the full-time help of half-wits'), *The New Yorker*, despite his pleas for cash, was paying him partly in stock, which wasn't worth much at the time. Mankiewicz drank heavily, and the drinking newspaperman was in the style of the *World* but not in the style of the *Times*. In October, 1925, he was almost fired. The drama critic then was Brooks Atkinson, and the drama editor was George S. Kaufman, with Mankiewicz second in line and Sam Zolotow third. Mankiewicz was sent to cover the performance of Gladys Wallis, who was the wife of the utilities magnate Samuel Insull, as Lady Teazle in *School for Scandal*. Mrs Insull, who had abandoned her theatrical career over a quarter of a century before, was, according to biographers, bored with being a nobody when her husband was such a big somebody. She was fifty-six when she resumed her career, as Lady Teazle, who is meant to be about eighteen. The play had opened in Chicago, where, perhaps astutely, she performed for charity (St Luke's Hospital), and the press had described her as brilliant. The night of the New York opening, Mankiewicz came back to the office drunk, started panning Mrs Insull's performance, and then fell asleep over his typewriter. As Zolotow recalls it, 'Kaufman began to read the review, and it was so venomous he was outraged. That was the only time I ever saw Kaufman lose his temper.' The review wasn't printed. The *Times* suffered the humiliation of running this item on October 23, 1925:

The *School for Scandal*, with Mrs Insull as Lady Teazle, was produced at the Little Theatre last night. It will be reviewed in tomorrow's *Times*.

Mankiewicz was in such bad shape that night that Kaufman told Zolotow to call Sara Mankiewicz and have her come get him and take him home. Mrs Mankiewicz recalls that he still had his head down on his typewriter when she arrived, with a friend, to remove him. She says he took it for granted that he was fired, but nevertheless went to work promptly the next day. Zolotow recalls, 'In the morning, Herman came down to the office and asked me to talk to Mr Birchall, the assistant managing editor, on his behalf. Herman had brought a peace offering of a bottle of Scotch and I took it to Birchall. He had a red beard, and he tugged at it and he stabbed the air a few times with his index finger and said, "Herman is a bad boy, a bad boy." But he took the bottle and Herman kept his job until he got the movie offer.'

The review – unsigned – that the *Times* printed on October 24, 1925, was a small masterpiece of tact:

As Lady Teazle, Mrs Insull is as pretty as she is diminutive, with a clear smile and dainty gestures. There is a charming grace in her bearing that makes for excellent deportment. But this Lady Teazle seems much too innocent, too thoroughly the country lass that Joseph terms her, to lend credit to her part in the play.

Scattered through various books, and in the stories that are still told of him in Hollywood, are clues that begin to give one a picture of Herman Mankiewicz, a giant of a man who mongered his own talent, a man who got a head start in the race to 'sell out' to Hollywood. The pay was fantastic. After a month in the movie business, Mankiewicz – though his Broadway shows had not been hits, and though this was in 1926, when movies were still silent – signed a year's contract giving him $400 a week and a bonus of $5,000 for each story that was accepted, with an option for a second year at $500 a week and $7,500 per accepted story, the company guaranteeing to accept at least four stories per year. In other words, his base pay was $40,800 his first year and $56,000 his second; actually, he wrote so many stories that he made much more. By the end of 1927, he was head of Paramount's scenario department, and in January, 1928, there was a newspaper item reporting that he was in New York 'lining up a new set of newspaper feature writers and playwrights to bring to Hollywood,' and that 'most of the newer writers on Paramount's staff who contributed the most successful stories of the past year were selected by "Mank."' One reason that Herman Mankiewicz is so little known today is, ironically, that he went to Hollywood so early, before he had gained a big enough reputation in the literary and theatrical worlds. Screenwriters don't make names for themselves; the most famous ones are the ones whose names were famous before they went to Hollywood, or who made names later in the theatre or from books, or who, like Preston Sturges, became directors.

Mankiewicz and other *New Yorker* writers in the twenties and the early thirties were very close to the world of the theatre; many of them were writing plays, writing about theatre people, reviewing plays. It's not surprising that within a few years the magazine's most celebrated contributors were in Hollywood writing movies. Of the ten friends of the editor Harold Ross who were in the original prospectus as advisory editors, six became screenwriters. When Mankiewicz gave up the drama critic's spot, in 1926, he was replaced by Charles Brackett, and when Brackett headed West, Robert Benchley filled it while commuting, and then followed. Dorothy Parker, the book reviewer Constant Reader, went West, too. Nunnally Johnson, who was to work on over a hundred movies, was a close friend of Harold Ross's and had volunteered to do the movie reviewing in 1926 but had been told that that job was for 'old ladies and fairies.' Others in the group didn't agree: Benchley had written on movies for the old *Life* as early as 1920, and John O'Hara later took time out from screenwriting to become the movie critic for *Newsweek* – where he was to review *Citizen Kane*. The whole group were interested in the theatre and the movies, and they were fast, witty writers, used to regarding their work not as deathless prose but as stories written to order for the market, used also to the newspaperman's pretense of putting a light value on what they did – the 'Look, no hands' attitude. Thus, they were well prepared to become the scenarists and gag writers of the talkies.

6

The comic muse of the most popular 'daring' late silents was a carefree, wisecracking flapper. Beginning in 1926, Herman Mankiewicz worked on an astounding number of films in that spirit. In 1927 and 1928, he did the titles (the printed dialogue and explanations) for at least twenty-five films that starred Clara Bow, Bebe Daniels, Nancy Carroll, Esther Ralston, George Bancroft, Thomas Meighan, Jack Holt, Richard Dix, Wallace Beery, and other public favorites. He worked on the titles for Jules Furthman's script of *Abie's Irish Rose*, collaborated with Anita Loos on the wisecracks for *Gentlemen Prefer Blondes*, and did the immensely successful *The Barker* and *The Canary Murder Case*, with William Powell, Louise Brooks, James Hall, and Jean Arthur. By then, sound had come in, and in 1929 he did the script as well as the dialogue for *The Dummy*, with Ruth Chatterton and Fredric March (making his screen début), wrote William Wellman's *The Man I Love*, with Richard Arlen, Pat O'Brien, and Mary Brian, and worked for Josef von Sternberg and many other directors.

Other screenwriters made large contributions, too, but probably none larger than Mankiewicz's at the beginning of the sound era, and if he was at that time one of the highest-paid writers in the world, it was because he wrote the kind of movies that were disapproved of as 'fast' and immoral. His heroes weren't soft-eyed and bucolic; he brought good-humored toughness to the movies, and energy and astringency. And the public responded, because it was eager for modern American subjects. Even those of us who were children at the time loved the fast-moving modern-city stories. The commonplaceness – even tawdriness – of the imagery was such a relief from all that silent 'poetry.' The talkies were a great step down. It's hard to make clear to people who didn't live through the transition how sickly and unpleasant many of those 'artistic' silent pictures were – how you wanted to scrape off all that mist and sentiment.

Almost from the time the motion-picture camera was invented, there had been experiments with sound and attempts at synchronization, and the public was more than ready for talking pictures. Many of the late silents, if one looks at them now, seem to be trying to talk to us, crying out for sound. Despite the legend of paralysis of the medium when sound first came in, there was a burst of inventiveness. In musicals, directors like René Clair and, over here, Ernst Lubitsch and, to a lesser degree, Rouben Mamoulian didn't use sound just for lip synchronization; they played with sound as they had played with images, and they tried to use sound without losing the movement of silents or the daring of silent editing. Some of the early talkies were static and inept; newly imported stage directors literally staged the action, as if the space were stage space, and the technicians had to learn to handle the microphones. But movies didn't suddenly become stagebound because of the microphone. Many of the silents had always been stagebound, for the sufficient reason that they had been adapted from plays – from the war-horses of the repertory, because they had proved their popularity, and from the latest Broadway hits, because the whole country wanted to see them. The silent adaptations were frequently deadly, not just because of construction based on the classical unities, with all those entrances and exits and that painful emptiness on the screen of plays worked out in terms of absolutely essential characters only, but because everything kept stopping for the explanatory titles and the dialogue titles.

Even in the movies adapted from novels or written directly for the screen, the action rarely went on for long; silents were choked with titles, which were perhaps, on the average, between ten and twenty times as frequent as the interruptions for TV commercials. The printed dialogue was often witty, and often it was essential to an understanding of the action, but it broke up the rhythm of performance and the visual flow, and the titles were generally held for the slowest readers, so that one lost the mood of the film while staring at the dialogue for the third scanning. (It seems to me, thinking back on it, that we were so eager for the movie to go on that we gulped the words down and then were always left with them for what, to our impatience, seemed an eternity, and that the better the movie, the more quickly we tried to absorb and leap past the printed words, and the more frustrating the delays became.) The plain fact that many silent movies were plays without the spoken dialogue, plays deprived of their very substance, was what made the theatre-going audience – and the Broadway crowd of writers – so contemptuous of them. Filmed plays without the actors' voices, and with the deadening delays for the heterogeneous audience to read the dialogue, were an abomination. Many of the journalists and playwrights and wits of the Algonquin Round Table had written perceptively about motion pictures (Alexander Woollcott, who managed to pan some of the greatest films, was an exception); they had, in general, been cynical only about the slop and the silent filmed plays. But though they had been active in the theatre, there had been no real place for them in movies; now, with the introduction of sound, they could bring to the screen the impudence that had given Broadway its flavor in the twenties – and bring it there before the satirical references were out of date. Sound made it possible for them to liberate movies into a new kind of contemporaneity.

7

There is an elaborate body of theory that treats film as 'the nocturnal voyage into the unconscious,' as Luis Buñuel called it, and for a director such as Buñuel 'the cinema seems to have been invented to express the life of the subconscious.' Some of the greatest work of D. W. Griffith and other masters of the silent film has a magical, fairy-tale appeal, and certainly Surrealists like Buñuel, and other experimental and avant-garde filmmakers as well, have drawn upon this dreamlike vein of film. But these artists were the exceptions; much of the dreamy appeal to the 'subconscious' and to 'universal' or 'primitive' fantasies was an appeal to the most backward, not to say reactionoary, elements of illiterate and semiliterate mass society. There was a steady load of calendar-art guck that patronized 'the deserving poor' and idealized 'purity' (i.e., virginity) and 'morality' (i.e., virginity plus charity). And all that is only one kind of movie anyway. Most of the dream theory of film, which takes the audience for passive dreamers, doesn't apply to the way one responded to silent comedies – which, when they were good, kept the audience in a heightened state of consciousness. When we join in laughter, it's as if the lights were on in the theatre. And not just the Mack Sennett comedies and Keaton and Chaplin kept us fully awake but the spirited, bouncy comediennes, like Colleen Moore and Marion Davies, and the romantic comedy 'teams,' and the suave, 'polished' villains, like William Powell. My favourite movies as a child were the Bebe Daniels comedies – I suppose they were the movie equivalent of the series books one reads at that age. During 1927 and 1928, Paramount brought a new one out every few months; Bebe, the athletic madcap, would fence like Douglas Fairbanks, or she would parody Valentino by kidnapping and taming a man, or she might be a daredevil newsreel camerawoman or a cub reporter.

I did not know until I started to look into the writing of *Citizen Kane* that the man who wrote *Kane* had worked on some of those pictures, too – that Mankiewicz had, in fact, written (alone or with others) about forty of the films I remember best from the twenties and thirties (as well as many I didn't see or don't remember). Mankiewicz didn't work on *every* kind of picture, though. He didn't do Westerns, and once, when a studio attempted to punish him for his customary misbehaviour by assigning him to a Rin Tin Tin picture, he turned in a script that began with the craven Rin Tin Tin frightened by a mouse and reached its climax with a house on fire and the dog taking a baby *into* the flames. I had known about Mankiewicz's contribution to *Kane* and a few other films, but I hadn't realized how extensive his career was. I had known that he was the producer of *Million Dollar Legs* (with W. C. Fields and Jack Oakie and Lyda Roberti) and *Laughter* (with Fredric March and Nancy Carroll), but I hadn't known, for example, that he had produced two of the Marx Brothers films that I've always especially liked, the first two made in Hollywood and written directly for the screen – *Monkey Business* and *Horse Feathers* – and part of *Duck Soup* as well. A few years ago, some college students asked me what films I would like to see again just for my own pleasure, and without a second's thought I replied *Duck Soup* and *Million Dollar Legs*, though at that time I had no idea there was any connection between them. Yet surely there is a comic spirit that links them – even the settings,

Freedonia and Klopstokia, with Groucho as Prime Minister of one and Fields as President of the other – and now that I have looked into Herman Mankiewicz's career it's apparent that he was a key linking figure in just the kind of movies my friends and I loved best.

When the period of the great silent comedians, with their international audience, was over, a new style of American comedy developed. One couldn't really call a colloquial, skeptical comedy a 'masterpiece,' as one could sometimes call a silent comedy a masterpiece, especially if the talkie looked quite banal and was so topical it felt transient. But I think that many of us enjoyed these comedies more, even though we may not have felt very secure about the aesthetic grounds for our enjoyment. The talking comedies weren't as aesthetically pure as the silents, yet they felt liberating in a way that even great silents didn't. The elements to which we could respond were multiplied; now there were vocal nuances, new kinds of timing, and wonderful new tricks, like the infectious way Claudette Colbert used to break up while listening to someone. It's easy to see why Europeans, who couldn't follow the slang and the jokes and didn't understand the whole satirical frame of reference, should prefer our action films and Westerns. But it's a bad joke on our good jokes that film enthusiasts here often take their cues on the American movie past from Europe, and so they ignore the tradition of comic irreverence and become connoisseurs of the 'visuals' and 'mises en scène' of action pictures, which are usually too silly even to be called reactionary. They're sub-reactionary – the antique melodramas of silent days with noise added – a mass art better suited, one might think, to Fascism, or even feudalism, than to democracy.

There is another reason the American talking comedies, despite their popularity, are so seldom valued highly by film aestheticians. The dream-art kind of film, which lends itself to beautiful visual imagery, is generally the creation of the 'artist'

director, while the astringent film is more often directed by a competent, unpretentious craftsman who can be made to look very good by a good script and can be turned into a bum by a bad script. And this competent craftsman may be too worldly and too practical to do the 'imaginative' bits that sometimes helped make the reputations of 'artist' directors. Ben Hecht said he shuddered at the touches von Sternberg introduced into *Underworld*: 'My head villain, Bull Weed, after robbing a bank, emerged with a suitcase full of money and paused in the crowded street to notice a blind beggar and give him a coin – before making his getaway.' That's exactly the sort of thing that quantities of people react to emotionally as 'deep' and as 'art,' and that many film enthusiasts treasure – the inflated sentimental with a mystical drip. The thirties, though they had their own load of sentimentality, were the hardest-headed period of American movies, and their plainness of style, with its absence of false 'cultural' overtones, has never got its due aesthetically.

Film students – and their teachers – often become interested in movies just because they are the kind of people who are emotionally affected by the blind-beggar bits, and they are indifferent by temperament to the emancipation of American movies in the thirties and the role that writers played in it.

I once jotted down the names of some movies that I didn't associate with any celebrated director but that had nevertheless stayed in my memory over the years, because something in them had especially delighted me – such rather obscure movies as *The Moon's Our Home* (Margaret Sullavan and Henry Fonda) and *He Married His Wife* (Nancy Kelly, Joel McCrea, and Mary Boland). When I looked them up, I discovered that Dorothy Parker's name was in the credits of *The Moon's Our Home* and John O'Hara's in the credits of *He Married His Wife*. Other writers worked on those films, too, and perhaps they were the ones who were responsible for what I responded to, but the recurrence of the names of that group of writers, not just on rather obscure remembered films but on almost *all* the films that are generally cited as proof of the vision and style of the most highly acclaimed directors of that period, suggests that the writers – and a particular group of them, at that – may for a brief period, a little more than a decade, have given American talkies their character.

8

There is always a time lag in the way movies take over (and broaden and emasculate) material from the other arts – whether it is last season's stage success or the novels of the preceding decade or a style or an idea that has run its course in its original medium. (This does not apply to a man like Jean-Luc Godard, who is not a mass-medium movie director.) In most productions of the big studios, the time lag is enormous. In the thirties, after the great age of musical comedy and burlesque, Hollywood, except for Paramount, was just discovering huge operettas. After the Broadway days of Clifton Webb, Fred Astaire, the Marx Brothers, Fanny Brice, W. C. Fields, and all the rest, M-G-M gave us Nelson Eddy and Jeanette MacDonald, and Universal gave us Deanna Durbin. This is the history of movies. J. D. Salinger has finally come to the screen through his imitators, and Philip Roth's fifties romance arrived at the end of the sixties. It may be that for new ideas to be successful in movies, the way must be prepared by success in other media, and the audience must have grown tired of what it's been getting and be ready for something new. There are always a few people in Hollywood who are considered mad dreamers for trying to do in movies things that have already been done in the other arts. But once one of them breaks through and has a hit, he's called a genius and everybody starts copying him.

The new spirit of the talkies was the twenties moved West in the thirties. George S. Kaufman was writing the Marx Brothers stage shows when he and Mankiewicz worked together at the *Times*; a little later, Kaufman directed the first Broadway production of *The Front Page*. Kaufman's collaborators on Broadway plays in the twenties and the early thirties included Marc Connelly, Edna Ferber, Ring Lardner, Morrie Ryskind, and Moss Hart as well as Mankiewicz – the nucleus of the Algonquin-to-Hollywood group. Nunnally Johnson says that the two most brilliant men he has ever known were George S. Kaufman and Herman Mankiewicz, and that, on the whole, Mankiewicz was the more brilliant of the two. I think that what Mankiewicz did in movies was an offshoot of the gag comedy that Kaufman had initiated on Broadway; Mankiewicz spearheaded the movement of that whole Broadway style of wisecracking, fast-talking, cynical-sentimental entertainment onto the national scene. Kaufman's kind of impersonal, visionless comedy, with its single goal of getting the audience to

29

laugh, led to the degeneration of the Broadway theatre, to its play doctors and gimmickry and scattershot jokes at defenseless targets, and so it would be easy to look down on the movie style that came out of it. But I don't think the results were the same when this type of comedy was transplanted to movies; the only bad long-range consequences were to the writers themselves.

Kaufman fathered a movement that is so unmistakably the bastard child of the arts as to seem fatherless; the gag comedy was perfectly suited to the commercial mass art of the movies, so that it appears to be an almost inevitable development. It suited the low common denominator of the movies even better than it suited the needs of the relatively selective theatre audience, and the basic irresponsibility of this kind of theatre combined with the screenwriters' lack of control over their own writing to produce what one might call the brothel period of American letters. It was a gold rush, and Mankiewicz and his friends had exactly the skills to turn a trick. The journalists' style of working fast and easy and working to order and not caring too much how it was butchered was the best kind of apprenticeship for a Hollywood hack, and they loved to gather, to joke and play games, to lead the histrionic forms of the glamorous literary life. Now they were gathered in cribs on each studio lot, working in teams side by side, meeting for lunch at the commissary and for dinner at Chasen's, which their old friend and editor Harold Ross had helped finance, and all over town for drinks. They adapted each other's out-of-date plays and novels, and rewrote each other's scripts. Even in their youth in New York, most of them had indulged in what for them proved a vice: they were 'collaborators' – dependent on the fun and companionship of joint authorship, which usually means a shared shallowness. Now they collaborated all over the place and backward in time; they collaborated promiscuously, and within a few years were rewriting the remakes of their own or somebody else's rewrites. Mankiewicz adapted Kaufman and Ferber's *The Royal Family* and *Dinner at Eight*, turned Alice Duer Miller's *Come Out of the Kitchen* into *Honey*, and adapted George Kelly's *The Show-Off* and James Thurber's *My Life and Hard Times* and works by Laurence Stallings and other old friends while Ben Hecht or Preston Sturges or Arthur Kober was working over something of his. They escaped the cold, and they didn't suffer from the Depression. They were a colony – expatriates without leaving the country – and their individual contributions to the script that emerged after the various rewrites were almost impossible to assess, because their attitudes were so similar; they made the same kind of jokes, because they had been making them to each other for so long. In Hollywood, they sat around building on to each other's gags, covering up implausibilities and dull spots, throwing new wisecracks on top of jokes they had laughed at in New York. Screenwriting was an extension of what they used to do for fun, and now they got paid for it. They had liked to talk more than to write, and this weakness became their way of life. As far as the official literary culture was concerned, they dropped from sight. To quote a classic bit of dialogue from Budd Schulberg's *The Disenchanted*:

'Bane had two hits running on Broadway at the same time. Even Nathan liked 'em. Popular 'n satirical. Like Barry, only better. The critics kept waiting for him to write that great American play.'
'What happened to him?'
'Hollywood.'

Hollywood destroyed them, but they did wonders for the movies. In New York, they may have valued their own urbanity too highly; faced with the target Hollywood presented, they became cruder and tougher, less tidy, less stylistically elegant, and more iconoclastic, and in the eyes of Hollywood they were slaphappy cynics, they were 'crazies.' They were too talented and too sophisticated to put a high value on what they did, too amused at the spectacle of what they were doing and what they were part of to be respected the way a writer of 'integrity,' like Lillian Hellman, was later to be respected – or, still later, Arthur Miller. Though their style was often flippant and their attitude toward form casual to the point of contempt, they brought movies the subversive gift of sanity. They changed movies by raking the old moralistic muck with derision. Those sickly Graustarkian romances with beautiful, pure high-born girls and pathetic lame girls and dashing princes in love with commoners, and all the Dumas and Sabatini and Blasco-Ibáñez, now had to compete with the freedom and wildness of American comedy. Once American films had their voice and the Algonquin group was turned loose on the scripts, the revolting worship of European aristocracy faded so fast that movie stars even stopped bringing home Georgian princes. In the silents, the heroes were often simpletons. In the talkies, the heroes were to be the men who weren't fooled, who were smart and learned their way around. The new heroes of the screen were created in the image of their authors: they were fast-talking newspaper reporters.

That Walter Burns whose entrance in *The Front Page* Kerr described was based on Walter Howey, who was the city editor of the *Chicago Tribune*, at $8,000 a year, until Hearst lured him away by an offer of $35,000 a year. Howey is generally considered the 'greatest' of all Hearst editors – by those who mean one thing by it, and by those who mean the other. He edited Hearst's *New York Mirror* at a time when it *claimed* to be ten per cent news and ninety per cent entertainment. The epitome of Hearstian journalism, and a favorite of Hearst's until the end, he was one of the executors of Hearst's will. At one time or another, just about all the Hollywood writers had worked for Walter Howey and/or spent their drinking hours with friends who did. He was the legend: the classic model of the amoral, irresponsible, irrepressible newsman who cares about nothing but scoops and circulation. He had lost an eye (supposedly in actual fighting of circulation wars), and Ben Hecht is quoted as saying you could tell which was the glass eye because it was the warmer one. Hecht used him again in *Nothing Sacred*, as Fredric March's editor – 'a cross between a Ferris wheel and a werewolf' – and he turns up under other names in other plays and movies. In a sense, all those newspaper plays and movies were already about Hearst's kind of corrupt, manic journalism.

The toughest-minded, the most satirical of the thirties pictures often featured newspaper settings, or, at least, reporters – especially the 'screwball' comedies, which had some resemblances to later 'black' comedy and current 'freaky' comedy but had a very different spirit. A newspaper picture meant a contemporary picture in an American setting, usually a melodrama with crime and political corruption and suspense and comedy and romance. In 1931, a title like *Five Star Final* or *Scandal Sheet* signalled the public that the movie would be a tough modern talkie, not a tearjerker with sound. Just to touch a few bases, there was *The Front Page* itself, in 1931, with Pat O'Brien as the reporter and Adolphe Menjou as Walter Burns; Lee Tracy as the gossip columnist in *Blessed Event* and as the press agent in *Bombshell*; Clark Gable as the reporter in *It Happened One Night*; Paul Muni giving advice to the lovelorn in *Hi, Nellie*; Spencer Tracy as the editor in *Libeled Lady*; Stuart Erwin as the correspondent in *Viva Villa!*; Jean Harlow stealing the affections of a newspaperman from girl reporter Loretta Young in *Platinum Blonde*; Jean Arthur as the girl reporter in *Mr Deeds Goes to Town*; a dozen pictures, at least, with George Bancroft as a Walter Howey-style bullying editor; all those half-forgotten pictures with reporter 'teams' – Fredric March and Virginia Bruce, or Joel McCrea and Jean Arthur, or Loretta Young and Tyrone Power (*Love Is News*); Cary Grant as the editor and Joan Bennett as the reporter in *Wedding Present*; and then Cary Grant as Walter Burns in *His Girl Friday*, with Rosalind Russell as the reporter; and then Cary Grant and James Stewart (who had been a foreign correspondent in *Next Time We Love*) both involved with a newsmagazine in *The Philadelphia Story*, in 1940. Which takes us right up to *Citizen Kane*, the biggest newspaper picture of them all – the picture that ends with the introduction of the cast and a reprise of the line 'I think it would be fun to run a newspaper.'

9

After years of swapping stories about Howey and the other werewolves and the crooked, dirty press, Mankiewicz found himself on story-swapping terms with the power behind it all, Hearst himself. When he had been in Hollywood only a short time, he met Marion Davies and Hearst through his friendship with Charles Lederer, a writer, then in his early twenties, whom Ben Hecht had met and greatly admired in New York when Lederer was still in his teens. Lederer, a child prodigy, who had entered college at thirteen, got to know Mankiewicz, the MacArthurs, Moss Hart, Benchley, and their friends at about the same time or shortly after he met Hecht, and was immediately accepted into a group considerably older than he was. Lederer was Marion Davies' nephew – the son of her sister Reine, who had been in operetta and musical comedy. In Hollywood, Charles Lederer's life seems to have revolved around his aunt, whom he adored. (Many others adored her also, though *Citizen Kane* was to give the world a different – and false – impression.) She was childless, and Lederer was very close to her; he spent a great deal of his time at her various dwelling places, and took his friends to meet both her and

Hearst. The world of letters being small and surprising, Charles Lederer was among those who worked on the adaptation of *The Front Page* to the screen in 1931 and again when it was remade as *His Girl Friday* in 1940, and, the world being even smaller than that, Lederer married Orson Welles' ex-wife, Virginia Nicholson Welles, in 1940, at San Simeon. (She married two prodigies in succession; the marriage to Welles had lasted five years and produced a daughter.)

Hearst was so fond of Lederer that on the evening of the nuptials he broke his rule of one cocktail to guests before dinner and no hard liquor thereafter. A guest who gulped the cocktail down was sometimes able to swindle another, but this is the only occasion that I can find recorded on which Hearst dropped the rule – a rule that Marion Davies customarily eased by slipping drinks to desperate guests before Hearst joined them but that nevertheless made it possible for Hearst to receive, and see at their best, some of the most talented alcoholics this country has ever produced. Not all writers are attracted to the rich and powerful, but it's a defining characteristic of journalists to be drawn to those who live at the center of power. Even compulsive drinkers like Mankiewicz and Dorothy Parker were so fascinated by the great ménage of Hearst and his consort – and the guest lists of the world-famous – that they managed to stay relatively sober for the evenings at Marion Davies' beach house (Colleen Moore described it as 'the largest house on the beach – and I mean the beach from San Diego to the Canadian border') and the weekends at San Simeon.

If *Kane* has the same love-hate as *The Front Page*, the same joyous infatuation with the antics of the unprincipled press, it's because Mankiewicz, like Hecht and MacArthur, revelled in the complexities of corruption. And Hearst's life was a *spectacle*. For short periods, this was intoxication enough. A man like Hearst seems to embody more history than other people do; in his company a writer may feel that he has been living in the past and on the outskirts and now he's living in the dangerous present, right where the decisions are really made.

Hearst represented a new type of power. He got his first newspaper in 1887, when he was twenty-four, by asking his father for it, and, in the next three decades, when, for the first time, great masses of people became literate, he added more and more papers, until, with his empire of thirty newspapers and fifteen magazines, he was the most powerful journalist and publisher in the world. He had brought the first comic strips to America in 1892, and his battling with Pulitzer a few years later over a cartoon character named the Yellow Kid revived the term 'yellow journalism.' Because there was no tradition of responsibility in this new kind of popular journalism, which was almost a branch of show business, Hearst knew no restraints; perhaps fortunately, he was unguided. Ultimately, he was as purposeless about his power as the craziest of the Roman emperors. His looting of the treasures of the world for his castle at San Simeon symbolized his imperial status. Being at his table was being at court, and the activities of the notables who were invited there were slavishly chronicled in the Hearst papers.

The new social eminence of the Mankiewiczes, who sometimes visited San Simeon for as long as ten days at a time, can be charted from Louella Parsons' columns. By the end of 1928, Louella was announcing Mankiewicz's writing assignments with a big bold headline at the top of the column, and was printing such items as:

> One of the few scenario writers in Hollywood who didn't have to unlearn much that he had learned is Herman Mankiewicz. Herman came to Paramount directly from the

stage, and naturally he knows the technique just as well as if he hadn't written movies in the interval.

It was worth another item in the same column that Herman Mankiewicz had been observed 'taking his son down Hollywood Boulevard to see the lighted Christmas trees.' In 1931, the Mankiewiczes were so prominent that they were among those who gave Marion Davies a homecoming party at the Hotel Ambassador; the other hosts were Mr and Mrs Irving Thalberg, Mr and Mrs King Vidor, Mr and Mrs Samuel Goldwyn, John Gilbert, Lewis Milestone, Hedda Hopper, and so on. Hedda Hopper, who worked as a movie columnist for a rival newspaper chain but was a close friend of Marion Davies (to whom, it is said, she owed her job), was also an enthusiastic reporter of Mankiewicz's activities during the years when he and his ravishing Sara were part of the Hearst-Davies social set.

When writers begin to see the powerful men operating in terms of available alternatives, while they have been judging them in terms of ideals, they often develop 'personal' admiration for the great bastards whom they have always condemned and still condemn. Hearst was to Mankiewicz, I suspect, what Welles was to be to him a little later – a dangerous new toy. And he needed new toys constantly to keep off the booze. Mankiewicz could control himself at San Simeon in the late twenties and the very early thirties, as, in those days, he could control himself when he was in charge of a movie. Producing the Marx Brothers comedies kept him busy and entertained for a while. With the title of 'supervisor' (a term for the actual working producer, as distinguished from the studio executive whose name might appear above or below the name of the movie), he worked on their pictures from the inception of the ideas through the months of writing and then the shooting. But he got bored easily, and when he started cutting up in the middle of preparing *Duck Soup*, in 1933, he was taken off the picture.

When the Marx Brothers left Paramount and went to M-G-M, he joined them again, in the preparation of *A Night at the Opera*, in 1935, and the same thing happened; he was replaced as supervisor by his old boss George S. Kaufman.

His credits began to taper off after 1933, and in 1936 Mankiewicz didn't get a single credit. That year, he published an article called 'On Approaching Forty,' a brief satirical account of what had happened to him as a writer. It began:

> Right before me, as I write, is a folder in which my wife keeps the blotters from Mr Eschner, the insurance man, Don's first report card, the letter from the income tax people about the gambling loss at Tia Juana, the press photograph of me greeting Helen Kane (in behalf of the studio) at the Pasadena Station and my literary output. There are four separate pieces of this output and they are all excellent. I hope some friend will gather them into a little book after my death. There is plenty of ninety point Marathon in the world, and wide margins can't be hard to find.

He includes those tiny pieces in their entirety, and after one of them – the first three sentences of a short story – he comments:

> I moved to Hollywood soon after I had made this notation and was kept so busy with one thing and another – getting the pool filled, playing the Cadillac and Buick salesmen against each other, only to compromise on a Cadillac and a Buick, after all, and locating the finance company's downtown office – that the first thing I knew, a story, a good deal like the one I had in mind, appeared in the *Saturday Evening Post*, and in *Collier's*, too.

This is the end of his article:

The fourth note looks rather naked now, all by itself on the desk. It says, simply:

'Write piece for *New Yorker* on reaching thirty-fifth birthday. No central idea. Just flit from paragraph to paragraph.'

People who complain that my work is slipshod would be a little surprised to find that I just am *not* always satisfied with the first thing I put down. I'm changing that thirty-fifth to fortieth right now.

'On Approaching Forty' didn't come out in *The New Yorker*; it appeared in the *Hollywood Reporter*.

Ambivalence was the most common 'literary' emotion of the screenwriters of the thirties, as alienation was to become the most common 'literary' emotion of the screenwriters of the sixties. The thirties writers were ambivalently nostalgic about their youth as reporters, journalists, critics, or playwrights, and they glorified the hard-drinking, cynical newspaperman. They were ambivalent about Hollywood, which they savaged and satirized whenever possible. Hollywood paid them so much more money than they had ever earned before, and the movies reached so many more people than they had ever reached before, that they were contemptuous of those who hadn't made it on their scale at the same time that they hated themselves for selling out. They had gone to Hollywood as a paid vacation from their playwriting or journalism, and screenwriting became their only writing. The vacation became an extended drunken party, and while they were there in the debris of the long morning after, American letters passed them by. They were never to catch up; nor were American movies ever again to have in their midst a whole school of the richest talents of a generation.

We in the audience didn't have to wake up *afterward* to how good those films of the thirties were; in common with millions of people, I enjoyed them while they were coming out. They were immensely popular. But I did take them for granted. There was such a steady flow of bright comedy that it appeared to be a Hollywood staple, and it didn't occur to me that those films wouldn't go on being made. It didn't occur to me that it required a special gathering of people in a special atmosphere to produce that flow, and that when those people stopped enjoying themselves those pictures couldn't be made. And I guess it didn't occur to older, more experienced people, either, because for decades everybody went on asking why Hollywood wasn't turning out those good, entertaining comedies anymore.

By the end of the thirties, the jokes had soured. The comedies of the forties were heavy and pushy, straining for humor, and the comic impulse was misplaced or lost; they came out of a different atmosphere, a different *feeling*. The comic spirit of the thirties had been happily self-critical about America, the happiness born of the knowledge that in no other country were movies so free to be self-critical. It was the comedy of a country that didn't yet hate itself. Though it wasn't until the sixties that the self-hatred became overt in American life and American movies, it started to show, I think, in the phony, excessive, duplicit use of patriotism by the rich, guilty liberals of Hollywood in the war years.

10

In the forties, a socially conscious film historian said to me, 'You know, Paramount never made a good movie,' and I brought up the names of some Paramount movies – *Easy Living* and *Trouble in Paradise* and lovely trifles like *Midnight* – and, of course, I couldn't make my point, because those movies weren't what was thought of in the forties as a good movie. I knew I wouldn't get anywhere at all if I tried to cite *Million Dollar Legs* or *Mississippi*, or pictures with the Marx Brothers or Mae West; I would be told they weren't even movies. Though

Paramount made some elegant comedies in the 'Continental' style, many of the best Paramount pictures were like revues – which was pretty much the style of the Broadway theatre they'd come out of, and was what I liked about them. They entertained you without trying to change your life, yet didn't congratulate you for being a slobbering bag of mush, either. But by the forties these were considered 'escapist entertainment,' and that was supposed to be *bad*. Many of the thirties comedies, especially the Paramount ones, weren't even 'artistic' or 'visual' movies – which is why they look so good on television now. They also sound good, because what that historian thought of as their irresponsibility is so much more modern than the sentimentalities of the war years. What was believed in was implicit in the styles of the heroes and heroines and in the comedy targets; the writers had an almost aristocratic disdain for putting beliefs into words. In the forties, the writers convinced themselves that they believed in everything, and they kept putting it all into so many bad words. It's no wonder the movies had no further use for a Groucho or a Mae West; one can imagine what either of them might have done to those words.

It's common to blame the McCarthyism of the fifties and the removal of blacklisted writers for the terrible, flat writing in American movies of recent years, but the writers might have recovered from McCarthyism (they might even have stood up to it) if they hadn't been destroyed as writers long before. The writing that had given American talkies their special flavor died in the war, killed not in battle but in the politics of Stalinist 'anti-Fascism.' For the writers, Hollywood was just one big crackup, and for most of them it took a political turn. The lost-in-Hollywood generation of writers, trying to clean themselves of guilt for their wasted years and their irresponsibility as *writers*, became political in the worst way – became a special breed of anti-Fascists. The talented writers, the major ones as well as the lightweight yet entertaining ones, went down the same drain as the clods – drawn into it, often, by bored wives, less successful brothers. They became naïvely, hysterically pro-Soviet; they ignored Stalin's actual policies, because they so badly needed to believe in something. They had been so smart, so gifted, and yet they hadn't been able to beat Hollywood's contempt for the writer. (Walter Wanger had put twenty-seven of them to work in groups in succession on the script of Vincent Sheean's *Personal History*.) They lived in the city where Irving Thalberg was enshrined; Thalberg, the saint of M-G-M, had rationalized Mayer's system of putting teams of writers to work simultaneously and in relays on the same project. It had been lunatic before, but Thalberg made it seem mature and responsible to fit writers into an assembly-line method that totally alienated them and took away their last shreds of pride. And most of the Algonquin group had been in Hollywood so long they weren't even famous anymore.

Talented people have rarely had the self-control to flourish in the Hollywood atmosphere of big money and conflicting pressures. The talented – especially those who weren't using their talents to full capacity – have become desperate, impatient, unreliable, self-destructive, and also destructive, and so there has always been some validity in the businessman's argument that he couldn't afford to take chances on 'geniuses.' Thalberg didn't play around with a man like Mankiewicz; after throwing him off *A Night at the Opera*, he didn't use him again.

The writers who had become accustomed to being assembly-line workers were ready to believe it when, in the forties, they were told that, like factory workers, they were 'part of the team on the assembly line' and needed 'the strengthening of the spirit which comes from identity with the labor of others.' Like the producers, the Screen Writers Guild respected discipline and responsibility, but though the businessmen had never been able to organize people of talent – producers like Thalberg just kept discarding them – the union ideologues knew how. The talented rarely become bureaucrats, but the mediocre had put down roots in Hollywood – it doesn't take long in Los Angeles, the only great city that is purely modern, that hasn't even an architectural past in the nineteenth century. In the forties, the talented merged with the untalented and became almost indistinguishable from them, and the mediocre have been writing movies ever since. When the good writers tried to regain their self-respect by becoming political activists in the Stalinist style, it was calamitous to talent; the Algonquin group's own style was lost as their voice blended into the preachy, self-righteous chorus.

The comedy writers who had laughed at cant now learned to write it and were rehabilitated as useful citizens of the community of mediocrity. It was just what the newly political congratulated themselves on – their constructive, uplifting approach – that killed comedy. When they had written frivolously, knowing that they had no control over how their writing would be used, or buried, or rewritten, they may have failed their own gifts and the dreams of their youth, but the work they turned out had human dimensions; they were working at less than full capacity, but they were still honest entertainers. Their humor was the humor of those trapped by human weakness as well as by 'the system,' and this was basic comedy – like the jokes and camaraderie of Army men. But when they became political in that morally superior way of people who are doing something for themselves but pretending it's for others, their self-righteousness was insufferable. They may have told lies in the themes and plots of the thirties comedies, but they didn't take their own lies seriously, they didn't *believe* their own lies, the way they did in the forties. In the forties, the Screen Writers Guild and the Hollywood Writers Mobilization (for wartime morale-building) held conferences at which 'responsible' writers brought the irresponsibles

43

into line. The irresponsibles were told they were part of an army and must 'dedicate their creative abilities to the winning of the war.' And, in case they failed to understand the necessity for didactic, 'positive' humor, there were panels and seminars that analyzed jokes and pointed out which ones might do harm. It was explained to the writers that 'catch-as-catch-can,' 'no-holds-barred' comedy was a thing of the past. 'A very funny line may make black-market dealings seem innocent and attractive,' they were told, and 'Respect for officers must be maintained at all times, in any scene, in any situation.'

Show-business people are both giddy and desperately, sincerely intense. When Stalinism was fashionable, movie people became Stalinists, the way they later became witches and warlocks. Apparently, many of the Hollywood Stalinists didn't realize they were taking any risks; they performed propaganda services for the various shifts in Russia's foreign policy and, as long as the needs of American and Russian policy coincided, this took the form of superpatriotism. When the war was over and the Cold War began, history left them stranded, and McCarthy moved in on them. The shame of McCarthyism was not only 'the shame of America' but the shame of a bunch of newly rich people who were eager to advise the world on moral and political matters and who, faced with a test, informed on their friends – and, as Orson Welles put it, not even to save their lives but to save their swimming pools. One might think that whatever they had gained emotionally from their activity they would have lost when they informed on each other, but it doesn't seem to have always worked that way. They didn't change their ideas when they recanted before the House Un-American Activities Committee; they merely gave in and then were restored to themselves. And they often seem to regard it not as their weakness but as their martyrdom. Show-business-Stalinism is basically not political but psychological; it's a fashionable form of hysteria and guilt that is by now not so much pro-Soviet as just abusively anti-American. America is their image of Hell (once again, because of Vietnam, they're in a popular position), and they go on being 'political' in the same way, holding the same faith, and for the same reasons, as in the late thirties and the forties. The restoration there is fairly general. In Hollywood recently, a man who used to be 'involved' told me he wanted to become more active again, and added, 'But, you know, I'm scared. The people who are urging me to do more are the same ones who ratted on me last time.'

Mankiewicz was too well informed politically to become a Communist Party-liner. Because he didn't support this line, he was – and only in part jokingly – considered a 'reactionary' by the activists of the Screen Writers Guild. Yet he went on to write the movie they point to with pride in Hollywood, the movie they all seem to feel demonstrates what *can* be done and what movies should be doing, and it's their all-time favorite because they understand it – and correctly – as a leftist film. Its leftism is, however, the leftism of the twenties and early thirties, before the left became moralistic. There were other expressions of the tough spirit of the thirties that came after the thirties were over. There may be a little of it in the newspaper film of the fifties *Sweet Smell of Success*, but the ambivalence there is harsher, grimmer, more artistically 'serious' than it was in the thirties; there's some in the happy mockery of Hollywood in *Singin' in the Rain*, which takes off from Kaufman and Hart's *Once in a Lifetime*, and in the films of Preston Sturges, who alone somehow managed to stay funny and tart. The only writer of this whole group who became a director with an individual style, Sturges kept American comedy alive single-handed through the mawkish forties. Maybe he was able to because he was a cynic and so politically baroque that he wasn't torn by doubts and guilts. The political show in Hollywood in the forties was just one more crazy scene to him; he'd grown up rich and eccentric in Europe, the son of that expatriate lady (called Mary in *The Loves of Isadora*) who gave Isadora Duncan the fatal scarf.

But Mankiewicz climaxed an era in *Kane*. He wrote a big movie that is untarnished by sentimentality, and it may be the only big biographical movie ever made in this country of which that can be said. *Kane* is unsanctimonious; it is without scenes of piety, masochism, or remorse, without 'truths' – in that period when the screenwriters were becoming so politically 'responsible' that they were using all the primitive devices to sell their messages, and movies once again became full of blind beggars, and omens of doom, and accidental death as punishment for moral and sexual infractions, and, of course, Maria Ouspenskaya seeing into people's hearts – the crone as guru.

11

Orson Welles wasn't around when *Citizen Kane* was written, early in 1940. Mankiewicz, hobbling about on a broken leg in a huge cast, was packed off – away from temptation – to Mrs Campbell's Guest Ranch, in Victorville, California, sixty-five miles from Los Angeles, to do the script. He had a nurse and a secretary to watch over him and John Houseman to keep him working, and they all lived there for about three months – in a combination dude ranch and rest home, where liquor was forbidden and unavailable – until the first draft of *Citizen Kane*, called simply and formidably *American*, was completed.

That insurance-company doctor who refused to accept Mankiewicz as a risk back in 1927 had no need to be prophetic. Ben Hecht once described a summer earlier in the twenties when he and his wife and Charles MacArthur were living in a borrowed house near Woodstock, New York, with no money, and Harpo, Groucho, Chico, and Zeppo Marx and their wives, sweethearts, and children came to stay, and then Herman Mankiewicz arrived, carrying two suitcases. 'He had decided to spend his vacation from the *New York Times* drama section with us,' Hecht wrote. 'He had not been allowed to bring any money with him because of Sara's certainty that he would spend it on liquor, and thus impair the influence of country air and sunshine. . . . Herman's larger suitcase contained sixteen bottles of Scotch and nothing else.' A few weeks later, Hecht and MacArthur went in to New York to try to sell a play they'd just written, and encountered Mankiewicz, who, having sent his wife and children out of town to escape the heat, was 'occupying Prince Bibesco's grand suite in the Plaza Hotel while His Highness capered in Long Island.'

Hecht went on, 'We moved in with him, there being no rent to pay. We discovered, while helping Herman to undress the first night, that his torso was bound with yards of adhesive tape. He had slipped while trying to get out of the bathtub and lamed his back. When Herman was alseep, MacArthur and I rolled him on his stomach and with an indelible pencil wrote ardent and obscene love messages on his taping. We signed them Gladys and chuckled over the impending moment in Far Rockaway when Herman would undress before his keen-eyed Sara.'

Not only was Mankiewicz alcoholic and maniacally accident-prone; he was a gambler, constantly in debt. There was a sequence in a thirties movie about a gambling newspaperman that was based on the way the other writers at Paramount used to line up with him when he got his check on Friday afternoon and walk with him to the bank so they could get back some of the money he'd borrowed from them during the week. His old friends say that he would bet from sheer boredom; when he ran out of big sporting events, he would bet on anything – on high-school football games or whether it would rain. He got to the point where he was bored with just betting; he wanted the stakes to be dangerously high. He once explained, 'It's not fun gambling if I lose two thousand and just write a check for it.

What's thrilling is to make out a check for fifteen thousand dollars knowing there's not a penny in the bank.' James Thurber referred to him as an 'incurable compulsive gambler.' He described how Mankiewicz went to a psychiatrist to see if anything could be done about it. 'I can't cure you of gambling,' the analyst told him on his last visit, 'but I can tell you why you do it.'

By the late thirties, Mankiewicz had just about run out of studios to get fired from. Scott Fitzgerald described him in those years as 'a ruined man.' His friends would get him jobs and he would lose them – sometimes in spectacular ways that became part of Hollywood legend. Perhaps the best-known is his exit from Columbia Pictures. In his biography of Harry Cohn, who was then the head of the studio, Bob Thomas describes it this way:

> The most famous incident in the Columbia dining room concerned an erratic genius named Herman J. Mankiewicz. . . . The free-wheeling world of journalism seemed better suited to his temperament than did Hollywood. He possessed two failings that were inimical to the autocratic studio domains: he drank, and he was scornful of his bosses.
>
> These faculties tumbled him from the position of a major screenwriter, and he had difficulty finding jobs. His agent, Charles Feldman, proposed a post at Columbia. Cohn was interested, since he enjoyed hiring bargain talent discarded by the major studios. . . . Cohn agreed to employ him at $750 a week.
>
> 'I want to make good,' said Mankiewicz when he reported to William Perlberg, then Columbia's executive producer.
>
> 'Fine,' said the producer. . . . 'But . . . don't go in the executive dining room. You know what will happen if you tangle with Cohn.'

Mankiewicz concurred. . . . His work habits were exemplary, and he produced many pages a day. But . . . his office was on the third floor, near the door to the executive dining room. As Riskin, Swerling, and other fellow-writers emerged after lunch, he could hear them laughing over wisecracks and jokes that had been told inside. Mankiewicz himself was considered one of Hollywood's premier wits and ranconteurs, and he rankled over his banishment.

One day Perlberg entered the dining room and was startled to find Mankiewicz sitting at the end of the table. The writer held a napkin to his mouth and promised, 'I won't say a word.'

When Cohn entered the room, he gave Mankiewicz a warm greeting, then assumed his monarchial position at the head of the table.

Cohn began the conversation: 'Last night I saw the lousiest picture I've seen in years.'

He mentioned the title, and one of the more courageous of his producers spoke up: 'Why, I saw that picture at the Downtown Paramount, and the audience howled over it. Maybe you should have seen it with an audience.'

'That doesn't make any difference,' Cohn replied. 'When I'm alone in a projection room, I have a foolproof device for judging whether a picture is good or bad. If my fanny squirms, it's bad. If my fanny doesn't squirm, it's good. It's as simple as that.'

There was a momentary silence, which was filled by Mankiewicz at the end of the table: 'Imagine – the whole world wired to Harry Cohn's ass!'

Mankiewicz's attitude toward himself and his work is summed up in one very short, very famous story. A friend who hadn't seen him for a while asked, 'How's Sara?'

Mankiewicz, puzzled: 'Who?'

'Sara. Your wife, Sara.'

'Oh, you mean Poor Sara.'

The only evidence of an instinct for self-preservation in the life of Herman Mankiewicz is his choice of keen-eyed Sara. He was in bad shape by 1939, but Mayer kept him on the payroll – some said so that top people at M-G-M could collect their gambling winnings from him. But Mayer also seems to have had some affection for him, and Sara had become a close friend of Mayer's daughter Irene. Mayer became concerned about Mankiewicz's gambling debts, and, assuming that Mankiewicz was also concerned about them, he concluded that if he got the debts straightened out, Mankiewicz would pull himself together. Mayer called him in and asked him how much money he needed to get financially clear. Mankiewicz came up with the figure of $30,000, and Mayer offered to advance him that sum on a new contract if he would swear a solemn vow never to gamble again. Mankiewicz went through an elaborate ritual of giving Mayer his sacred word, and walked out with the $30,000. The very next day, it is said, Mankiewicz was playing poker on the lot, and he had just raised the stakes to $10,000 when he looked up and saw Mayer standing there. Mankiewicz left the studio and didn't return. A few days after that – early in September of 1939 – Thomas Phipps, a nephew of Lady Astor's, who was also employed as a writer at M-G-M, was driving to New York to court a lady there, and, with nothing better to do, Mankiewicz decided to go along. As Mankiewicz described the trip some months later, in a guest column he wrote, filling in for Hedda Hopper on vacation, it was fairly giddy right from the start. Mankiewicz said that each song on the car radio sent Phipps swooning, because either he had heard it while he was with his lady or he had heard it while he was not with her. On the outskirts of Albuquerque, the car skidded and turned over. Mankiewicz's jocular account included at the climax 'thirty-four weeks in a cast in bed and thirty-two weeks in a brace.' Phipps had a broken collarbone; when it healed, he proceeded on his romantic way to New York. Mankiewicz had a compound fracture of the left leg, which, together with further injuries suffered while the fracture was healing, left him with a limp for the rest of his life.

During the long recuperation – very long, because on his first night out on the town after his cast was removed, he went on crutches to Chasen's, got drunk, slipped and broke more bones, and had to be put in another cast – Mankiewicz, bedridden and in exile from the studios, began to write the Mercury Theatre's 'Campbell Playhouse' radio shows, with the actors often gathered around his bed for story conferences, and even rehearsals. Welles, having come to Hollywood in July to fulfill his contract with Schaefer, had been flying to and from New York for the series; in October he arranged to have the shows originate in Los Angeles, and in November he hired Mankiewicz to write five of them. Welles had met Mankiewicz sometime earlier in New York. This is John Houseman's recollection of those events, set down in a letter to Sara Mankiewicz after her husband's death:

I remember so well the day Orson came back to the theatre from '21', telling me he had met this amazingly civilized and charming man. I can just see them there at lunch together – magicians and highbinders at work on each other, vying with each other in wit and savoir-faire and mutual appreciation. Both came away enchanted and convinced that, between them, they were the two most dashing and gallantly intelligent gentlemen in the Western world. And they were not so far wrong! Soon after that I met Herman myself, but I didn't get to know him until . . . he lay in bed at Tower Road, his leg in a monstrous plaster cast . . . and we started to do those pecular collaborative radio shows in the beginning of our long conspiracy of love and hate for

Maestro, the Dog-Faced Boy. Then came *Kane* and Victorville and those enchanted months of inhabiting Mrs Campbell's ranch with our retinue of nurse and secretary and our store of Mickey Finns!

Tower Road was where the Mankiewiczes lived and the Mercury group gathered. The Dog-Faced Boy is, of course, Orson Welles (Cocteau once described him as 'a dog who has broken loose from his chain and gone to sleep on the flower bed'), and the Mickey Finns were a medical concoction that was supposed to make Mankiewicz hate alcohol. It failed. The secretary, Mrs Rita Alexander (she lent her name to the character of Susan Alexander), recalls that during her first week, before Sara Mankiewicz had had a chance to give her a briefing, Mankiewicz persuaded her to take him in to the town of Victorville, where he could get a drink. She withstood his wiles after that. He really wasn't in condition to do much drinking; the broken bones included a hip break, and he was in such poor condition that even eating presented problems. Mrs Alexander recalls spoon-feeding him bicarbonate of soda, and recalls his courtly, formal apologies for the belches that rocked the room.

12

There are monsters, and there are also sacred monsters; both Welles and Mankiewicz deserve places in the sacred-monster category. Some writers on film – particularly in England – blithely say that Kane wasn't based on Hearst, using as evidence statements that Welles made to the press in early 1941, when he was trying to get the picture released. But those who think Louella Parsons got the *mistaken* idea that the picture was about Hearst don't understand what kind of man the young Welles was. Welles and Mankiewicz wanted to do something startling, something that would cap the invasion of the Martians – which had, after all, panicked only the boobs, and inadvertently at that, though Welles now makes it sound deliberate. This time, he and Mankiewicz *meant* to raise cain. The pun is surely theirs, and Hearst had walked right into it; he was so fond of a story called *Cain and Mabel*, which he'd bought and produced as a Cosmopolitan Picture back in 1924, that he remade it late in 1936, at Warners', starring Clark Gable and Marion Davies. It had been one of her last pictures before her retirement. Cain and Mabel – it was a perfect description of Hearst and Marion. In 1960, when Welles was interviewed on British television, he said, 'Kane isn't really founded on Hearst in particular.' I suppose he was feeling rather expansive at that moment, and it may have seemed to limit his importance if his Kane had been based on anyone 'in particular.' In the same interview, he said, 'You asked me did Mr Hearst try to stop it. *He* didn't. . . . He was like Kane in that he wouldn't have stooped to such a thing.' This was rather droll, but Welles seemed to mean it. He didn't seem to know much about Hearst anymore; probably he'd forgotten. One may also fairly conclude that Welles, with that grandeur which he seems to have taken over from the theatre into his personal life, was elevating Hearst, lending Hearst some of his own magnitude. More characteristically, however, his grandeur is double-edged, as in this typical statement on Gregg Toland:

I had a great advantage not only in the real genius of my cameraman but in the fact that he, like all men who are masters of a craft, told me at the outset that there was nothing about camerawork that any intelligent being couldn't learn in half a day. And he was right.

Welles was thus telling us that he learned all there was to know about camerawork in half a day. What, one wonders, was the craft that Toland needed to master? Welles, like Hearst,

53

and like most very big men, is capable of some very small gestures. And so was Mankiewicz, who brought his younger, more stable brother, Joe, out to Hollywood and helped him get started, but, as soon as Joe had some success, began behaving atrociously, referring to him as 'my idiot brother.'

Mankiewicz's ambivalence was generally on a higher level, however. There are many different kinds of senses of humor, and the one that sometimes comes through Mankiewicz anecdotes is the perverse soul of Kane himself. There is, for example, the story that Ezra Goodman tells in *The Fifty Year Decline and Fall of Hollywood*. Hollywood was not often elegant and correct, but the producer Arthur Hornblow, Jr. was known for the punctiliousness of his social functions. At a dinner party that he gave for Hollywood notables, Herman Mankiewicz drank too much and threw up on the table. 'A deadly hush descended over the assembled guests. . . . Mankiewicz broke the silence himself: "It's all right, Arthur; the white wine came up with the fish."'

The man who in those circumstances could put his host down was a fit companion for Welles. They were big eaters, big talkers, big spenders, big talents; they were not men of what is ordinarily called 'good character.' They were out to get not only Hearst but each other. The only religious remark that has ever been attributed to Mankiewicz was recorded on the set of *Citizen Kane*: Welles walked by, and Mankiewicz muttered, 'There, but for the grace of God, goes God.'

13

Herman Mankiewicz didn't – to be exact – write *Citizen Kane*; he dictated it. The screenwriters may have felt like whores and they may have been justified in that feeling, but they were certainly well-paid whores. In New York, they hadn't had secretaries, but the movie business was mass culture's great joke on talent. The affectation of 'Look, no hands' became the literal truth. Mankiewicz dictated the script while the nurse watched over him and John Houseman stood by in attendance. This was a cut-rate job – Mankiewicz was getting $500 a week for his ghostly labors – but it was still in the royal tradition of screenwriting. Outside the movie business, there has probably never been a writer in the history of the world who got this kind of treatment. There was an urgency about it: Welles and most of the Mercury Theatre company were in Hollywood doing their weekly radio shows and waiting while this odd little group spent the spring of 1940 in Victorville preparing the script for Orson Welles' début in films.

Welles had come to Hollywood the previous July in a burst of publicity, but his first two film projects hadn't got under way. Within a few months of his arrival, he was being jeered at because nothing had happened. Although his contract with R.K.O. gave him freedom from interference, Schaefer and his legal staff had to approve the project and clear the shooting script and, of course, the budget. It had been agreed that his first project would be Conrad's *Heart of Darkness*, which he had already done as a radio drama. He was to play both Marlow and Kurtz, the two leading roles, and it was reported in the trade press that he was working on the script with John Houseman and Herbert Drake, who was the Mercury's press agent. In the latter part of 1939, Welles brought actors out from New York and shot long test sequences, but the budget looked too high to the poverty-stricken studio, and the production was repeatedly postponed. He decided to do something while he was waiting – something that he could start on right away, to get the Mercury actors on the R.K.O. payroll – and he hit on a spy thriller with a political theme: *The Smiler with the Knife*, from the novel by Nicholas Blake (C. Day Lewis). Welles adapted the book himself – 'in seven days,' according to the trade press – but this project was abandoned almost at once because of differences with Schaefer over

55

casting. (Welles wanted to use Lucille Ball, then a contract player at R.K.O., in the lead, and Schaefer didn't think she could carry the picture. As the whole world knows, she wound up owning the studio, but Schaefer wasn't necessarily wrong; she never did carry a picture.) There was still hope for *Heart of Darkness* – and a lot of money had already been spent on it – but things seemed to be falling apart for the Mercury group. By the end of 1939, Welles was desperate for a subject that would be acceptable to R.K.O. The movie plans were up in the air, and there was dissension within the Mercury group about staying on in Hollywood with nothing definite in sight to work on. Some of the actors left to take jobs elsewhere, and some were beginning to get film roles – a development that upset Welles, because he wanted them to be 'new faces' in his first film.

A policy meeting was arranged to discuss the failing fortunes of the group and to decide whether to keep them all in Los Angeles or send some of them back to New York. The more or less administrative heads of the Mercury Theatre met for dinner in an upper room at Chasen's. The group included Welles; Houseman, who had founded the Mercury Theatre with him; two all-purpose assistants, Richard Wilson and William Alland; the press agent, Drake; and several others. Houseman argued that the actors should return to New York, but nothing had been settled by the time the coffee and brandy arrived, and then Welles, in a sudden access of rage, shouted that Houseman wanted to desert him, that Houseman had always been against him, and he threw the coffee warmers – full of Sterno canned heat – at Houseman. He did not throw them very precisely, it seems; he threw them not so much with intent to hit as in Houseman's general direction. Dave Chasen, having been summoned by a waiter, opened the door, and, with the aplomb he had used back in the thirties in vaudeville, when he was the stooge of the comedian Joe Cook, he took one look – a curtain was on fire by then – and closed the door. The men in the room stamped out the fire, and Houseman went home and sent Welles a letter of resignation. The partnership was ended, and a week later Houseman left for New York.

Welles' tantrum and how it ended the partnership that had created the Mercury Theatre was the talk of the actors who gathered around Mankiewicz's bed, and it must have registered on Mankiewicz in a special way: it must have practically thrust on him the recognition of an emotional link between Welles and William Randolph Hearst, whose tantrums had been the stuff of legend among newspapermen for half a century, and whose occasional demonstrations of childishness were the gossip of guests at San Simeon. A week or two after the Chasen's dinner party, Mankiewicz proposed to Welles that they make a 'prismatic' movie about the life of a man seen from several different points of view. Even before he went to work in Hollywood and met Hearst, when he was still at the *New York Times*, Mankiewicz was already caught up in the idea of a movie about Hearst. Marion Fisher, the Mankiewicz baby-sitter, whose family lived in the same Central Park West building, was learning to type in high school and Mankiewicz offered to 'test her typing.' He dictated a screenplay, organized in flashbacks. She recalls that he had barely started on the dictation, which went on for several weeks, when she remarked that it seemed to be about William Randolph Hearst, and he said, 'You're a smart girl.' Mankiewicz couldn't pay her but she and her parents saw about fifty shows on the theatre tickets he gave them, and it was a great year for Broadway – 1925. Although in the intervening years Mankiewicz had often talked to friends about what a movie Hearst's life would make, his first suggestions to Welles for the 'prismatic' movie were Dillinger and, when Welles was cool to that, Aimee Semple McPherson. Only after Welles had rejected that, too, and after they had discussed the possibilities in the life of Dumas, did he propose

Hearst. Mankiewicz must have been stalling and playing games to lead Welles on, because although he was interested in both Dillinger and Aimee Semple McPherson, and subsequently did prepare scripts on them, this movie had to be a starring vehicle for Welles, and what major role could Welles play in the life of either Dillinger or Aimee? From what Mankiewicz told friends at the time, when he sprang the name Hearst, Welles leaped at it.

Welles had grown up hearing stories about Hearst from Dr Maurice Bernstein, who was his guardian after his parents died. Dr Bernstein was a good friend of Ashton Stevens, who had originally been the drama critic on Hearst's flagship paper, the *San Francisco Examiner*, and had gone on to work for Hearst in Chicago. Welles himself was a Hearst-press 'discovery'; it was Ashton Stevens, whom Dr Bernstein got in touch with, who had publicized the nineteen-year-old Orson Welles when he produced *Hamlet* on a vacant second floor in Illinois. But Welles, being a knowledgeable young man, would have known a great deal about Hearst even without this personal connection, for Hearst was the unifying hatred of all liberals and leftists. Welles, with his sense of the dramatic, would have known at once what a sensational idea a movie about Hearst was. Aimee and Dillinger just didn't have the dimensions that Hearst had; Hearst was even right for Welles *physically*. Welles and Mankiewicz must have enjoyed thinking what a scandal a movie about him would make. Mankiewicz didn't need to have misgivings about repercussions, because the risks would all be Welles'. Schaefer had signed Welles up to a widely publicized four-way contract as producer, director, writer, and actor. It was understood that he would take the credit for the script, just as he did for the scripts of the radio plays. His R.K.O. contract stated that 'the screenplay for each picture shall be written by Mr Orson Welles,' and Welles probably took this stipulation as no more than his due – a necessity of his station. He probably accepted the work that others did for him the way modern Presidents accept the work of speech-writers.

The title *American* suggests how Mankiewicz felt about the project. Several years before, in 1933, his friend and drinking companion Preston Sturges had written a big one, an original called *The Power and the Glory*, which, when it was produced, with Spencer Tracy and Colleen Moore in the leading roles, made Tracy a star. *The Power and the Glory* was about a ruthless railroad tycoon who fails in his personal life, and it was told in flashbacks and narration from his funeral. It was an impressive picture, and it was lauded in terms similar to those later used about *Kane*. 'Its subject,' William Troy wrote in the *Nation*, 'is the great American Myth, and its theme is futility.' The ballyhoo included putting a bronze tablet in the New York theatre where it opened to commemorate 'the first motion picture in which narratage was used as a method of telling a dramatic story.' (Hollywood, big on ballyhoo but short on real self-respect, failed to transfer the nitrate negative to safety stock, and modern prints of *The Power and the Glory* are tattered remnants.) Not only is the tycoon treated ambivalently by Sturges but in the boyhood sequence he is injured through his own arrogance, so that he acquires a jagged, lightninglike scar on his hand – the mark of Cain. The idea of the big-businessman as a Cain figure was basic to this genre, which had become popular in the Depression thirties, when many business giants of the twenties were revealed to be swindlers, or, at the very least, ruthless. In another 1933 film, *I Loved a Woman*, a tycoon's mistress sang at the Chicago Opera House. (It was where the tycoons' mistresses did sing in the twenties.) In 1937, Mankiewicz himself had done a trial run on the tycoon theme (with Edward Arnold as a lumber baron) in *John Meade's Woman*. To do Hearst, a much more dangerous man – the only tycoon who was also a demagogue – in a technique similar to Sturges's but from several different points of view would make a really big picture.

But there was a sizable hurdle: How could they get R.K.O. to approve this project? Welles and Mankiewicz went on talking about it for a couple of weeks, while Mankiewicz continued writing the weekly radio shows. When they decided to go ahead and try to slip it over on the studio somehow, Welles still had to find a way to get Mankiewicz to do the writing; the Mercury company couldn't be kept waiting in Los Angeles indefinitely while Mankiewicz wandered loose. Mankiewicz had had to be hauled off to sanatoriums to be dried out too many times for Welles to take chances, and the screenwriters who had worked with Mankiewicz at Metro told too many stories about his losing interest in the scripts he was assigned to and drinking so much during working hours that the other writers would load him into a studio car in mid-afternoon and have the driver haul him home, where Sara would unload him and put him to bed, and he would sleep it off before dinner and be ready for the night's drinking. He had just injured himself again, in his fall at Chasen's, and his bones were being reset, but soon he would be off on the town once more, despite cast or crutches, and there would be no way to hold him down to work. Welles hit on the scheme of packing Mankiewicz off to the country to recuperate. In early January, 1940, Welles flew to New York, and over lunch at '21' the young magician prevailed on Houseman to return to the Coast and do him and the Mercury one last service by running herd on Mankiewicz; only a month had passed since the fiery scene at Chasen's. (It was to be not the last but the next-to-last collaborative project of Welles and Houseman. A week after *American* was done and the troupe had left Victorville, Houseman and Welles were on bad terms again, but Mankiewicz, who was said to have read every new book by publication date, even when he was in the worst possible shape, told them that they'd be crazy if they didn't buy a new book that was just coming out, and dramatize it. Houseman went to work on it, and as a result Richard Wright's *Native Son* was adapted for the stage and produced so quickly that Welles had it playing in New York by the time *Citizen Kane* opened.)

Both Houseman and Mankiewicz unquestionably had mixed feelings about Welles by the time they found themselves at the guest ranch. Houseman admits that right from the beginning, when Mankiewicz started on the script, they planned to have Welles re-enact his tantrum. It was set for the scene in which Susan leaves Kane (Welles' wife, Virginia, had brought suit for divorce during the month Welles had his tantrum), and Mankiewicz wrote it up rather floridly and with explicit directions, in a passage beginning, 'Kane, in a truly terrible and absolutely silent rage . . .' When it was time to shoot the scene, the various members of the group who had been at Chasen's – or had heard about what happened there, and everybody *had* – encouraged Welles to do what he had done that night. Last year, William Alland, describing the making of the film in an interview printed in the magazine of the Directors Guild of America, said:

There was one scene which stands out above all others in my memory; that was the one in which Orson broke up the roomful of furniture in a rage. Orson never liked himself as an actor. He had the idea that he should have been feeling more, that he intellectualized too much and never achieved the emotion of losing himself in a part.

When he came to the furniture-breaking scene, he set up four cameras, because he obviously couldn't do the scene many times. He did the scene just twice, and each time he threw himself into the action with a fervor I had never seen in him. It was absolutely electric; you felt as if you were in the presence of a man coming apart.

Orson staggered out of the set with his hands bleeding and his face flushed. He almost swooned, yet he was exultant. 'I really felt it,' he exclaimed. 'I really felt it!'

Strangely, that scene didn't have the same power when it appeared on the screen. It might have been how it was cut, or because there hadn't been close-in shots to depict his rage. The scene in the picture was only a mild reflection of what I had witnessed on that movie stage.

Writing that scene into the movie was a cruel trick on Welles, designed to make him squirm. He had been built up so much that he was by then the white hope (as it used to be called) of the theatre. In 1938, even George S. Kaufman and Moss Hart had taken him to be that; they had written one of their worst maudlin 'serious' plays (and a flop) – *The Fabulous Invalid*, a cavalcade-of-the-American-theatre sort of play – and had modelled its hero on Welles. The hero – the leader of a new acting company – made a classic final curtain speech to his actors:

We haven't got very much money, but we've got youth and, I think, talent. They'll tell you the theatre is dying. I don't believe it. Anything that can bring us together like this, and hold us to this one ideal in spite of everything, isn't going to die. They'll tell you it isn't important, putting makeup on your face and playacting. I don't believe it. It's important to keep alive a thing that can lift men's spirits above the everyday reality of their lives. We mustn't let that die. Remember – you're going to be kicked around, and a lot of the time you're not going to have enough to eat, but you're going to get one thing in return. The chance to write, and act, say the things you want to say, and do the things you want to do. And I think that's enough.

For the people who did much of the work on Welles' projects, the temptation must have been strong to expose what they considered this savior's feet of clay.

The menagerie at Mrs Campbell's being scarcely a secret, they had many visitors (Welles himself came to dinner once or twice), and several of these visitors, as well as Houseman and Mrs Alexander, describe how Herman Mankiewicz turned out the script that became *Citizen Kane*. Mankiewicz couldn't go anywhere without help; he sat up, in the cast that covered one leg and went up to his middle, and played cribbage with Mrs Alexander during the day, while telling her stories about Hearst and Marion Davies and San Simeon. Then, at night, from about eight-thirty to eleven-thirty or twelve, he dictated, and she would type it out so he could have it the next day. Mrs Alexander recalls that during the first days on the job, when she was fascinated by the romantic significance of 'Rosebud' and asked him how the story would turn out, he said, 'My dear Mrs Alexander, I don't know. I'm making it up as I go along.' Welles was so deeply entangled in the radio shows and other activities and a romance with Dolores Del Rio at the time the script was being prepared that even when he came to dinner at Victorville, it was mainly a social visit; the secretary didn't meet him until after Mankiewicz had finished dictating the long first draft. Welles probably made suggestions in his early conversations with Mankiewicz, and since he received copies of the work weekly while it was in progress at Victorville, he may have given advice by phone or letter. Later, he almost certainly made suggestions for cuts that helped Mankiewicz hammer the script into tighter form, and he is known to have made a few changes on the set. But Mrs Alexander, who took the dictation from Mankiewicz, from the first paragraph to the last, and then, when the first draft was completed and they all went back to Los Angeles, did the secretarial work at Mankiewicz's house on the rewriting and the cuts, and who then handled the script at the studio until after the film was shot, says that Welles didn't write (or dictate) one line of the shooting script of *Citizen Kane*.

Toward the end of the period at the ranch, Mankiewicz began to realize that he'd made a very bad financial deal, and that the credit might be more important than he'd anticipated. After talks with Mrs Alexander and the Mercury people who visited on weekends, he decided he was going to get screen credit, no matter what his bargain with Welles had been. Meanwhile, Houseman, who says that according to his original agreement to go off to the ranch he was supposed to get some kind of credit, discovered once again, and as so many others had, that it wasn't easy to get your name on anything Orson Welles was involved in. Houseman was apparently fed up with arguments, and he says he waived his claim when he saw how determined Welles was; he left for New York and got started on the preparations for *Native Son*. But Mankiewicz was an experienced Hollywood hand and veteran of credit brawls who kept all his drafts and materials, and a man who relished trouble. He had ample proof of his authorship, and he took his evidence to the Screen Writers Guild and raised so much hell that Welles was forced to split the credit and take second place in the listing.

At the time the movie came out, Mankiewicz's contribution to the film was generally known. The screen credit was to Herman J. Mankiewicz and Orson Welles. The *Hollywood Reporter* simplified the credit to 'Written by Herman Mankiewicz'; Burns Mantle, in his newspaper column, referred to Mankiewicz's having written it; and, of course, Ben Hecht explained to the readers of *PM*, 'This movie was not written by Orson Welles. It is the work of Herman J. Mankiewicz.' In that period, it was well known that if the producer of a film wanted a screenplay credit it was almost impossible to prevent him from getting it. So many producers took a writing credit as a *droit du seigneur* for a few consultations or suggestions that the Screen Writers Guild later instituted a rule calling for compulsory arbitration whenever a producer sought a credit. Under the present rules of the Guild, Welles' name would probably not have appeared. And so it was by an awful fluke of justice that when Academy Awards night came, and Welles should have got the awards he deserved as director and actor, the award he got (the only Academy Award he has ever got) was as co-author of the Best Original Screenplay.

14

The Mercury group weren't surprised at Welles' taking a script credit; they'd had experience with this foible of his. Very early in his life as a prodigy, Welles seems to have fallen into the trap that has caught so many lesser men – believing his own publicity, believing that he really was the whole creative works, producer-director-writer-actor. Because he *could* do all these things, he imagined that he *did* do them. (A Profile of him that appeared in *The New Yorker* two years before *Citizen Kane* was made said that 'outside the theatre . . . Welles is exactly twenty-three years old.') In the days before the Mercury Theatre's weekly radio shows got a sponsor, it was considered a good publicity technique to build up public identification with Welles' name, so he was credited with just about everything, and was named on the air as the writer of the Mercury shows. Probably no one but Welles believed it. He had written some of the shows when the program first started, and had also worked on some with Houseman, but soon he had become much too busy even to collaborate; for a while Houseman wrote them, and then they were farmed out. By the time of the *War of the Worlds* broadcast, on Halloween, 1938, Welles wasn't doing any of the writing. He was so busy with his various other activities that he didn't always direct the rehearsals himself, either – William Alland or Richard Wilson or one of the other Mercury assistants did it. Welles might not come in until the last day, but somehow, all agree, he would pull the show together 'with a magic touch.' Yet when the Martian broadcast became accidentally famous, Welles seemed to forget that Howard Koch had written it. (In all the furor over the broadcast, with front-page stories everywhere, the name of the author of the radio play wasn't mentioned.) Koch had been writing the shows for some time. He lasted for six months, writing about twenty-five shows altogether – working six and a half days a week, and frantically, on each one, he says, with no more than half a day off to see his family. The weekly broadcasts were a 'studio presentation' until after the *War of the Worlds* (Campbell's Soup picked them up then), and Koch, a young writer, who was to make his name with the film *The Letter* in 1940 and win an Academy Award for his share in the script of the 1942 *Casablanca*, was writing them for $75 apiece. Koch's understanding of the agreement was that Welles would get the writing credit on the air for publicity purposes but that Koch would have any later benefit, and the copyright was in Koch's name. (He says that it was, however, Welles' idea that he do the Martian show in the form of radio bulletins.) Some years later, when C.B.S. did a program about the broadcast and the panic it had caused, the network re-created parts of the original broadcast and paid Koch $300 for the use of his material. Welles sued C.B.S. for $375,000, claiming that he was the author and that the material had been used without his permission. He lost, of course, but he may still think he wrote it. (He frequently indicates as much in interviews and on television.)

'Foible' is the word that Welles' former associates tend to apply to his assertions of authorship. Welles could do so many different things in those days that it must have seemed almost accidental when he didn't do things he claimed to. Directors, in the theatre and in movies, are by function (and often by character, or, at least, disposition) cavalier toward other people's work, and Welles was so much more talented and magnetic than most directors – and so much younger, too – that people he robbed of credit went on working with him for years, as Koch went on writing more of the radio programs after Welles failed to mention him during the national publicity about the panic. Welles was dedicated to the company, and he was exciting to work with, so the company stuck together, working for love, and even a little bit more money (Koch was raised to $125 a show) when they got a sponsor and, also as a result of the *War of the Worlds* broadcast, the movie contract that took them to Hollywood.

If there was ever a young man who didn't need unearned credits, it was Orson Welles, yet though he was already too big, he must have felt he needed to dazzle the world. Welles was hated in Hollywood long before he'd made a movie; he was hated almost upon his arrival. Form time to time, Hollywood used to work up considerable puerile resentment against 'outsiders' who dared to make movies. The scope of Welles' reputation seems to have infuriated Hollywood; it was a cultural reproach from the East and the Hollywood people tried to protect themselves by closing ranks and making Welles a butt of their humor. Gene Lockhart composed a stupid, nasty ditty called 'Little Orson Annie,' which was sung at Hollywood parties; the name stuck and was used by the columnists, though Hedda Hopper supported him and suggested that Hollywood reserve judgment, and Louella Parsons, on December 31st, selected him as 'the most discussed personality to come to the films in 1939.' Yet for Welles, with his beard (he was growing it for the Shakespearean production he intended to stage as soon as he could pick up his Hollywood loot), to be ensconced in the Mary Pickford-

Buddy Rogers estate, right next door to Shirley Temple, was too much for Hollywood. Welles became the victim of practical jokers. One night when he was dining at Chasen's, an actor cut off his tie with a table knife. Not all the jokes were so Freudian, but they were mostly ugly. Welles had come with an unprecedented contract. Probably the old Hollywoodians not only expected him to fall on his face but hoped he would, so that their mediocrity and prosperity would be vindicated. But Welles was the braggart who makes good. And, despite their resentment, they *were* dazzled by *Citizen Kane*.

15

The picture got a thunderous reception, even in the Hollywood press. In recent years, the rumor has spread that *Citizen Kane* opened to bad reviews – presumably on the theory that it was so far ahead of its time that it wasn't understood – and this is now recorded in many film histories. But it was very well understood by the press (who would understand a newspaper picture better?), and it got smashing reviews. It isn't, after all, a difficult picture. In some ways, it was probably better understood then than it is now, and, as far as I can determine, it was more highly praised by the American press than any other movie in history. The New York opening of *Citizen Kane*, which had been scheduled for February 14, 1941, finally took place on May 1st, and a week later it opened in Los Angeles. In January, Hedda Hopper had 'doubted' whether the picture would ever be released, and some of the trade press had predicted that it wouldn't be. Possibly it wouldn't have been except for the screenings that Welles arranged and the publicity that he got.

The whole industry was already involved in the picture. Although technically Welles had the right of final cut, the editor, Robert Wise, was instructed by the studio, with Welles' consent, to take a print to New York in January. Wise ran it for the heads of all the major companies and their lawyers, and for six weeks he and his then assistant, Mark Robson, who was on the Coast, fussed over the movie, making tiny, nervous changes – mostly a word here or there – that the executives and lawyers hoped would render the picture less objectionable to Hearst. Meanwhile, Schaefer had engaged Time, Inc.'s legal specialist on invasion-of-privacy suits; the lawyer instructed Schaefer that if he made one small cut in the film, no one could win such a suit. The dangerous section was a bit of dialogue by Raymond, the butler, suggesting that the old man was senile. Schaefer says he had no difficulty persuading Welles to agree to the cut. However, at the beginning of March, Hearst sent for Walter Howey, and no one was sure what they might be poking into. 'Nor are private lives to be overlooked,' Hedda Hopper predicted; and her predictions were the same as threats. Hearst's maneuvers were in the true Kane spirit: In January, Hedda Hopper had warned that 'the refugee situation would be looked into,' which meant that there would be pressure for a legal review of whether various imported stars and directors should be allowed to remain in the country, and the industry would be attacked for employing foreigners; that is, refugees from Hitler. Three days after the press previews, the Hearst newspapers, the American Legion, the Veterans of Foreign Wars, and other patriotic organizations went into action to rid radio of 'subversives.' The 'subversives' they were after were William Saroyan, Maxwell Anderson, Marc Connelly, Robert E. Sherwood, Stephen Vincent Benét, Paul Green, Sherwood Anderson, and James Boyd, who were involved with Welles in a series of C.B.S. radio plays on the general theme of freedom, which, although it had been encouraged by the Justice Department, was now condemned as un-American and as tending to promote Communism. Before *Citizen Kane* was released, *PM* reported that Hearst photographers were following Welles 'in G-man style,' trying to get something on him, while *Variety* reported 'persistent inquiries at the draft board as to why Welles hadn't been drafted.' It was along about this time that Hearst himself saw the picture. Schaefer says, 'Hearst personally sent to me at the studio and asked to see a print, and we let him have it. This was before it opened. There was no response, no comment. Orson knew this.' Welles may have feared that Schaefer would buckle unless he squeezed him from the other side, or, as Schaefer claims, it may have been Welles' way of getting more publicity, but, for whatever reason, Welles began to issue threats: he gave R.K.O. the deadline of March 30th for releasing the picture or facing a lawsuit. On March 11th, Welles called a press conference to alert the press to the danger that the film might be suppressed, and gave out this statement:

I believe that the public is entitled to see *Citizen Kane*. For me to stand by while this picture was being suppressed would constitute a breach of faith with the public on my part as producer. I have at this moment sufficient financial backing to buy *Citizen Kane* from R.K.O. and to release it myself. Under my contract with R.K.O. I have the right to demand that the picture be released and to bring legal action to force its release. R.K.O. must release *Citizen Kane*. If it does not do so immediately, I have instructed my attorney to commence proceedings.

I have been advised that strong pressure is being brought to bear in certain quarters to cause the withdrawal of my picture *Citizen Kane* because of an alleged resemblance between incidents in the picture and incidents in the life of Mr William Randolph Hearst.

Any such attempts at suppression would involve a serious interference with freedom of speech and with the integrity of the moving picture industry as the foremost medium of artistic expression in the country.

There is nothing in the facts to warrant the situation that has arisen. *Citizen Kane* was not intended to have nor has it any reference to Mr Hearst or to any other living person. No statement to the contrary has ever been authorized by me. *Citizen Kane* is the story of a wholly fictitious character.

The script for *Citizen Kane* was scrutinized and approved by both R.K.O. Radio Pictures and the Hayes office. No one in those organizations nor anyone associated with me in the production of the picture believed that it represented anything but psychological analysis of an imaginary individual. I regret exceedingly that anyone should interpret *Citizen Kane* to have a bearing upon any living person, or should impugn the artistic purposes of its producers.

Several of the magazines responded to his plea for the pressure of publicity by reviewing the picture before it opened, obviously with the intention of helping to get it released. A review in *Time* on March 17, 1941, began:

As in some grotesque fable, it appeared last week that Hollywood was about to turn upon and destroy its greatest creation.

It continued:

To most of the several hundred people who have seen the film at private showings, *Citizen Kane* is the most sensational product of the U.S. movie industry. It has found important new techniques in picture-making and story telling. ... It is as psychiatrically sound as a fine novel. . . . It is a work of art created by grown people for grown people.

In *Newsweek*, also on March 17, 1941, John O'Hara began his review with

> It is with exceeding regret that your faithful bystander reports that he has just seen a picture which he thinks must be the best picture he ever saw.
>
> With no less regret he reports that he has just seen the best actor in the history of acting.
>
> Name of picture: *Citizen Kane*.
>
> Name of actor: Orson Welles.
>
> Reason for regret: you, my dear, may never see the picture.
>
> I saw *Citizen Kane* the other night. I am told that my name was crossed off a list of persons who were invited to look at the picture, my name being crossed off because some big shot remembered I had been a newspaperman. So, for the first time in my life, I indignantly denied I was a newspaperman. Nevertheless, I had to be snuck into the showing of *Citizen Kane* under a phony name. That's what's going on about this wonderful picture. Intrigue.
>
> Why intrigue? Well, because. A few obsequious and/or bulbous middle-aged ladies think the picture ought not to be shown, owing to the fact that the picture is rumored to have something to do with a certain publisher, who, for the first time in his life, or maybe the second, shall be nameless. That the nameless publisher might be astute enough to realize that for the first time in his rowdy life he had been made a human being did not worry the loyal ladies. Sycophancy of that kind, like curtseying, is deliberate. The ladies merely wait for a chance to show they can still do it,

even if it means cracking a femur. This time I think they may have cracked off more than they can chew. I hope.

Along the way, O'Hara said such things as

My intention is to make you want to see the picture; if possible, to make you wonder why you are not seeing what I think is as good a picture as was ever made. . . . And aside from what it does not lack, *Citizen Kane* has Orson Welles. It is traditional that if you are a great artist, no one gives a damn about you while you're still alive. Welles has had plenty of that. He got a tag put to his name through the Mars thing, just as Scott Fitzgerald, who wrote better than any man in our time, got a Jazz Age tag put to his name. I say, if you plan to have any grandchildren to see and to bore, see Orson Welles so that you can bore your grandchildren with some honesty. There never has been a better actor than Orson Welles. I just got finished saying there never has been a better actor than Orson Welles, and I don't want any of your lip.

Do yourself a favor. Go to your neighborhood exhibitor and ask him why he isn't showing *Citizen Kane*.

The same day – March 17, 1941 – *Life*, which was to run several more features on the movie in the following months, came out with four pages of pictures and a review:

Few movies have ever come from Hollywood with such powerful narrative, such original technique, such exciting photography. Director Welles and Cameraman Gregg Toland do brilliantly with a camera everything Hollywood has always said you couldn't do. They shoot into bright lights, they shoot into the dark and against low ceilings, till every scene comes with the impact of something never seen before. Even the sound track is new. And for narrative Welles has tapped a segment of life fearfully skirted by the U.S. cinema: the swift and brutal biography of a power-mad newspaper tycoon, a man of twisted greatness who buys or bullies his way into everything but friends' love and his nation's respect. To a film industry floundering in a rut, *Citizen Kane* offers enough new channels to explore for five years to come.

Hearst must have known he would be in for a bad time if the picture should be withheld; the Luce magazines – *Time* and *Life* – had always been eager to embarrass him, and certainly wouldn't let the subject drop. (The financial backing that Welles said he had to buy the picture was probably from Henry Luce.) One surmises that Hearst decided not to try to block its release – though the petty harassment of R.K.O. and others involved went on, like a reflex to a blow.

Here is a representative selection from the reviews:

Variety: A film possessing the sure dollar mark.

Times (Bosley Crowther): Suppression of this film would have been a crime. . . . *Citizen Kane* is far and away the most surprising and cinematically exciting motion picture to be seen here in many a moon. . . . It comes close to being the most sensational film ever made in Hollywood.

Herald Tribune (Howard Barnes): A young man named Orson Welles has shaken the medium wide-awake with his magnificent film, *Citizen Kane*. His biography of an American dynast is not only a great picture; it is something of a revolutionary screen achievement. . . . From any standpoint *Citizen Kane* is truly a great motion picture.

Post (Archer Winsten): It goes without saying this is the picture that wins the majority of 1941's movie prizes in a walk, for it is inconceivable that another will come along to challenge it. . . . Orson Welles with this one film establishes himself as the most exciting director now working. . . . Technically the result marks a new epoch.

PM (Cecelia Ager): Before *Citizen Kane*, it's as if the motion picture was a slumbering monster, a mighty force stupidly sleeping, lying there sleek, torpid, complacent – awaiting a fierce young man to come kick it to life, to rouse it, shake it, awaken it to its potentialities, to show it what it's got. Seeing it, it's as if you never really saw a movie before: no movie has ever grabbed you, pummelled you, socked you on the button with the vitality, the accuracy, the impact, the professional aim, that this one does.

Esquire (Gilbert Seldes): Welles has shown Hollywood how to make movies. . . . He has made the movies young again, by filling them with life.

Cue (Jesse Zunser): It is an astounding experience to watch Orson Welles, 25-year-old Boy Genius of the Western World, in the process of creating on the screen one of the awesome products of his fertile imagination. You come away limp, much as if you had turned into Broadway and suddenly beheld Niagara Falls towering behind the Paramount Building, the Matterhorn looming over Bryant Park, and the Grand Canyon yawning down the middle of Times Square.

Hollywood Reporter: A great motion picture. . . . A few steps ahead of anything that has been made in pictures before.

Chicago Journal of Commerce (Claudia Cassidy): Anyone who has eyes in his head and ears to hear with will enjoy *Citizen Kane* for the unleashed power of its stature on the screen.

Even Kate Cameron, in the *Daily News*, gave it four stars, and on Sunday, May 4th, Bosley Crowther (though he had some second thoughts of his own) wrote in the *Times*, 'The returns are in from most of the local journalistic precincts and Orson Welles' *Citizen Kane* has been overwhelmingly selected as one of the great (if not the greatest) motion picture of all time. . . .' The *Film Daily* said, 'Welles can prepare his mantel for a couple of Oscars.'

16

Had it not been for the delays and the nervous atmosphere that made the picture *seem* unpopular and so *become* unpopular, it might have swept the Academy Awards. It had taken the New York Film Critics Award with ease, but early in 1942, when the 1941 Academy Awards were given, the picture had the aroma of box-office failure – an aroma that frightens off awards in Hollywood. The picture had been nominated in nine categories, and at the ceremony, each time the title or Orson Welles' name was read, there were hisses and loud boos. The prize for the Original Screenplay was perhaps partly a love gesture to Herman Mankiewicz, one of their own; the film community had closed ranks against Orson Welles.

While the picture was being shot, Welles, like a good showman, had done his best to preserve the element of surprise, and he had been smart about keeping a tight, closed set. He didn't want interference from anybody, and even though the R.K.O. executives had read the script, when one of them 'dropped in' once to see what was going on, Welles coolly called a halt in the shooting, and the Mercury players went outside and played baseball until he left. There were visitors, of course. Invitations to attend the first official day of shooting were sent to the press, and Welles was simply careful about what he shot that day. And the crew didn't go out to play baseball when Louella Parsons visited the set a few weeks later; they were just very careful, so that even though she had heard rumors that the picture was about Hearst, everything looked so innocent and Welles denied the rumors so disarmingly that she went on giving him an enthusiastic press. (She later described his outfoxing her on this occasion as 'one of the classic double crosses of Hollywood.') But Mankiewicz, with his 'Don't let this get around,' was practically incapable of keeping a secret. He was so proud of his script that he lent a copy to Charles Lederer. In some crazily naïve way, Mankiewicz seems to have imagined that Lederer would be pleased by how good it was. But Lederer, apparently, was deeply upset and took the script to his aunt and Hearst. It went from them to Hearst's lawyers (who marked various passages) before it was returned to Mankiewicz, and thus Hearst and his associates were alerted early to the content of the film. It was probably as a result of Mankiewicz's idiotic indiscretion that the various forces were set in motion that resulted in the cancellation of the première at the Radio City Music Hall, the commercial failure of *Citizen Kane*, and the subsequent failure of Orson Welles. This was how, even before the film was finished, Hearst's minions were in action, and how there was time for Mayer and his people to set about their attempt to suppress the film, and, having failed in that, to destroy it commercially.

In the aftermath of the presssures, and of the disappointing returns on the film, the members of the Academy could feel very courageous about the writing award. Mankiewicz had become a foolhardy hero in taking on Hearst; *Kane* was Mankiewicz's finest moment. They wanted him to have a prize; he deserved it and he needed it. Hollywood loves the luxury of show-business sentimentality, and Hollywood loves a comeback. The members of the Academy destroyed Orson Welles that night, but they probably felt good because their hearts had gone out to crazy, reckless Mank, their own resident loser-genius, the has-been who was washed up in the big studios, who was so far down he had been reduced to writing Welles' radio shows. At the beginning of the thirties, he had been earning $4,000 a week; at the end of the thirties, he was a ghost. What they couldn't know was that *Kane* was Welles' finest moment, too; the reason they couldn't know it was that their failure to back him that night was the turning point. Welles had made *Citizen Kane* at twenty-five, and he seemed to have the world before him. They'd had time to get used to Mank's self-destructiveness, and he'd been down on his luck so long he was easy to love; besides, they admired the pranks that had got him thrown out of one studio after another. Welles was self-destructive in a style they weren't yet accustomed to.

One may speculate that if the members of the Academy had supported Welles and voted *Citizen Kane* Best Picture of the Year, if they had backed the nation's press and their own honest judgment, the picture might have got into the big theatrical showcases despite the pressures against it. If they had, *Kane* might have made money, and things might have gone differently for Welles – and for American movies. The Academy had plenty of sentiment but not enough guts. And so Orson Welles peaked early. Later, as his situation changed and his fortunes sank and *Kane* became the golden opportunity of his youth, his one great chance of freedom to accomplish something, then, when he looked back, he may really have needed to believe what he was quoted as saying in France: 'Le seul film que j'aie jamais écrit du premier au dernier mot et pu mener à bien est *Citizen Kane*.' The literal translation is 'The only film that I ever wrote from first word to last and was able to bring to a successful issue is *Citizen Kane*,' but I think that what it means is 'The picture came out well.' What else can it mean when one considers the contributions of Mankiewicz and Toland and all the rest? Men cheated of their due are notoriously given to claiming more than their due. The Academy members had made their token gesture to *Citizen Kane* with the screenplay award. They failed what they believed in; they gave in to the scandal and to the business pressures. They couldn't yet know how much guilt they *should* feel: guilt that by their failure to support *Citizen Kane* at this crucial time – the last chance to make *Kane* a financial success – they had started the downward spiral of Orson Welles, who was to become perhaps the greatest loser in Hollywood history.

17

Like D. W. Griffith, Orson Welles came into the movies in order to make money so that he could continue in the theatre, and, like Griffith, he discovered that movies were the medium in which he could do what he had barely dreamed of doing in the theatre. Soon – even before he started on *Citizen Kane* – Welles was desperate for money to make movies. It took guile to get *Kane* approved. Robert Wise, whom the head of the R.K.O. editing department had assigned to the picture because he was close to Welles' age, says, 'Orson sneaked the project onto R.K.O. He told the studio that he was merely shooting tests.' Sets were built, and shooting began on June 29, 1940; the 'test shots' were fully produced. The Mercury actors and associates were there anyway, most of them under personal contract to Welles, as Mankiewicz was. But Dorothy Comingore, not a member of the Mercury Theatre but a Hollywood bit player (who, as Linda Winters, had worked in Westerns and with the Three Stooges and in Blondie and Charlie Chan pictures), says that she lived on unemployment checks of $18 a week while she 'tested for one month' for the role of Susan Alexander. She adds, 'All these tests were incorporated into the film; they were never retaken.' After a month, with the studio buzzing about how brilliant the footage was, the movie was practically a *fait accompli*, and

Welles was able to bulldoze Schaefer into approving the project. All the people who were alreaady at work on *Citizen Kane* – the cameraman, the grips, the composer, the assistants, and the actors – met at Herman Mankiewicz's house for breakfast, and Welles announced that the picture had been approved and could formally begin. They officially started on July 30, 1940, and they finished 'principal photography' eighty-two shooting days later, on October 23, 1940, even though Welles – almost as accident-prone as Mankiewicz – broke his ankle during the scene when he ran down the stairs from Susan's room while yelling that he'd get Boss Gettys.

Yet it took more than guile to function in the motion-picture business at that time. It helped to be mercenary, of course, but what really counted then was not to care *too* much about your work. After *Citizen Kane*, the contract that gave Welles the right of final cut was cancelled, so he did not have control of *The Magnificent Ambersons*, and it was shortened and mangled. The industry was suspicious of him, and not just because of the scandal of *Kane*, and the general fear of Hearst, and *Kane*'s unsatisfactory financial returns. Alva Johnston described the Hollywood attitude toward Welles in an article in the *Saturday Evening Post* in 1942, the year after *Kane* came out:

Big agents soon lost interest in the boy genius. They learned that he wasn't interested in money. Welles became known as a dangerous Red because, when his first picture project was shelved after the studio had wasted a good deal of money on it, he offered to make another picture for nothing.

Genius got a bad name on account of Welles. It was brought into complete disrepute by Saroyan. The gifted Armenian came to Hollywood with a small agent and insisted on working without a salary, leaving it to M-G-M to set a value on his services after his work was completed. He said, 'I'll trust the studio.' The $10,000,000-a-year agency business is wholly based on the motto 'Don't trust the studio.' Since the Welles and Saroyan affairs, it has been practically impossible to interest a big agent in an intellectual giant.

When you write straight reporting about the motion-picture business, you're writing satire. Motion-picture executives prefer to do business with men whose values they understand. It's very easy for these executives – businessmen runing an art – to begin to fancy that they are creative artists themselves, because they are indeed very much like the 'artists' who work for them, because the 'artists' who work for them are, or have become, businessmen. Those who aren't businessmen are the Hollywood unreliables – the ones whom, it is always explained to you, the studios can't hire, because they're crazy. As soon as movies became Welles' passion, and he was willing to work on any terms, he was finished in the big studios – they didn't trust him. And so, somehow, Welles aged before he matured – and not just physically. He went from child prodigy to defeated old man, though today, at fifty-five, he is younger by a decade or two than most of the big American directors.

In later years, Welles, a brilliant talker, was to give many interviews, and as his power in the studios diminished, his role in past movies grew larger. Sometimes it seems that his only power is over the interviewers who believe him. He is a masterful subject. The new generation of film historians have their own version of 'Look, no hands': they tape-record interviews. Young interviewers, particularly, don't bother to check the statements of their subjects – they seem to regard that as outside their province – and thus leave the impression that the self-aggrandizing stories they record are history. And so, as the years go on, if one trusts what appears in print,

Welles wrote not only *Kane* but just about everything halfway good in any picture he ever acted in, and in interviews he's beginning to have directed anything good in them, too. Directors are now the most interviewed group of people since the stars in the forties, and they have told the same stories so many times that not only they believe them, whether they're true or false, but everybody is beginning to.

This worship of the director is cyclical – Welles or Fellini is probably adored no more than von Stroheim, or von Sternberg or De Mille was in his heyday – but such worship generally doesn't help in sorting out what went into the making of good pictures and bad pictures. The directors try to please the interviewers by telling them the anecdotes that have got a good response before. The anecdotes are sometimes charming and superficial, like the famous one – now taken for motion-picture history – about how Howard Hawks supposedly discovered that *The Front Page* would be better if a girl played the reporter Hildy, and thus transformed the play into *His Girl Friday* in 1940. ('I was going to prove to somebody that *The Front Page* had the finest modern dialogue that had been written, and I asked a girl to read Hildy's part and I read the editor, and I stopped and I said, "Hell, it's better between a girl and a man than between two men."') Now, a charming story is not nothing. Still, this is nothing but a charming and superficial story. *His Girl Friday* turned out joyously, but if such an accident did cause Hawks to see how easy it was to alter the play, he still must have done it rather cynically, in order to make it conform to the box-office patterns then current. By the mid-thirties – after the surprise success of *It Happened One Night* – the new independent, wisecracking girl was very popular, especially in a whole cycle of newspaper pictures with rival girl and boy reporters. Newspaper pictures were now 'romantic comedies,' and, just as the movies about lady fliers were almost all based on Amelia Earhart, the criminal-mouthpiece movies on William Fallon, and the gossip-column movies on Walter Winchell, the movies about girl reporters were almost all based on the most highly publicized girl reporter – Hearst's Adela Rogers St Johns. Everybody had already been stealing from and unofficially adapting *The Front Page* in the 'wacky' romantic newspapers comedies, and one of these rewrites, *Wedding Present*, in 1936 (by Adela Rogers St Johns' then son-in-law Paul Gallico), had tough editor (Cary Grant) and smart girl reporter (Joan Bennett) with square fiancé (Conrad Nagel). This was the mold that *The Front Page* was then squeezed into to become *His Girl Friday*, with Cary Grant, Rosalind Russell, and Ralph Bellamy (already a favorite square from *The Awful Truth*) in the same roles, and Rosalind Russell was so obviously playing Adela Rogers St Johns that she was dressed in an imitation of the St Johns girl-reporter striped suit.

Some things that students now, seeing films out of the context of the cycles they were part of, may take to be brilliant inventions were fairly standard; in fact, the public at the time was so familiar with the conventions of the popular comedies that the clichés were frequently spoofed within the pictures. But today, because of the problems peculiar to writing the history of modern mass-art forms, and because of the jumbled circumstances in which movies survive, with knowledge of them acquired in haphazard fashion from television, and from screenings here and there, film enthusiasts find it simpler to explain movies in terms of the genius-artist-director, the schoolbook hero – the man who did it all. Those who admire *Citizen Kane*, which is constructed to present different perspectives on a man's life, seem naïvely willing to accept Welles' view of its making; namely, that it is his sole creation.

Howard Hawks must wonder what the admiration of the young is worth when he learns from them that he invented overlapping dialogue in *His Girl Friday*, since it means that they have never bothered to look at the text of the original Hecht and MacArthur play. Welles, too, has been said to have invented overlapping dialogue, and just about everything else in *Kane*. But unearned praise is insulting, and a burden; Welles sometimes says, 'I drag my myth around with me.' His true achievements are heavy enough to weigh him down. Welles is a great figure in motion-picture history: he directed what is almost universally acclaimed as the greatest American film of the sound era; he might have become the greatest all-around American director of that era; and in his inability to realize all his artistic potentialities he is the greatest symbolic figure in American film history since Griffith.

18

In the past few years, I have heard two famous 'artist' directors, after showings of their early films, explain how it happened that in the screen credits there was someone else listed for the script. It seems there was this poor guy on the lot who needed a credit desperately, and the company asked the director if he'd give the stumblebum a break; the incompetent turned in some material, but the director couldn't use any of it. Some listeners must swallow this, because in the latest incense-burning book on Josef von Sternberg the screen credits are simply ignored, and he, rather than Ben Hecht, is listed as the author of *Underworld*. Herman J. Mankiewicz has been similarly dropped from one film after another. The directors' generosity to those poor credit-hungry guys seems to have cut-off points in time (the directors' creative roles get bigger when the writers are dead) and in space (when the directors are interviewed abroad). Orson Welles, however, didn't need time or distance; he omitted any mention of his writer right from the start. (This custom is now being followed by many directors.) In later years, when he has been specifically asked by interviewers whether Mankiewicz wrote the scenario for *Citizen Kane*, he has had a set reply. 'Everything concerning Rosebud belongs to him,' he has said. Rosebud is what was most frequently criticized in the movie, and Gilbert Seldes, in one of the most solid and intelligent reviews of *Kane* (in *Esquire*), called it 'a phony' and 'the only bit of stale stuff in the picture.' Welles himself has said, 'The Rosebud gimmick is what I like least about the movie. It's a gimmick, really, and rather dollar-book Freud.'

Welles may have been goaded into malice; he had probably never come up against a man so well equipped to deal with him as Mankiewicz. Welles, who used to tell stories about how when he was seventeen he became a *torero* in Seville and entered several *corridas* and was billed on the posters as 'The American,' may have got a few welts, starting with Mankiewicz's original title – *American*. When Welles read the script, he must certainly have recognized what he was caught in. There's no doubt that Welles – the fabulous Orson Welles – wasn't accustomed to sharing credit. However, his persistent lack of generosity toward Mankiewicz started at the time the movie came out, and it may have its basis in a very specific grievance. Mankiewicz may have outsmarted Welles on the credits more than once. Nunnally Johnson says that while *Citizen Kane* was being shot, Mankiewicz told him that he had received an offer of a ten-thousand-dollar bonus from Welles (through Welles' 'chums') to hold to the original understanding and keep his name off the picture. Mankiewicz said that Welles had been brooding over the credits, that he could see how beautiful they would be: 'Produced by Orson Welles. Directed by Orson Welles. Starring Orson Welles.' It was perfect until he got to 'Herman J. Mankiewicz' in the writing credit, which spoiled everything. Mankiewicz said he was tempted by Welles' offer. As usual, he needed money, and, besides, he was fearful of what would happen when the picture came out – he might be blackballed forever. William

Randolph Hearst, like Stalin, was known to be fairly Byzantine in his punishments. At the same time, Mankiewicz knew that *Citizen Kane* was his best work, and he was proud of it. He told Johnson that he went to Ben Hecht with his dilemma, and that Hecht, as prompt with advice as with scripts, said, 'Take the ten grand and double-cross the son of a bitch.'

I asked Nunnally Johnson if he thought Mankiewicz's story was true, and Mankiewicz actually had got the offer and had taken Hecht's advice. Johnson replied, 'I like to believe he did.' It's not unlikely. Mankiewicz wrote the first draft in about three months and tightened and polished it into the final shooting script of *Citizen Kane* in a few more weeks, and he probably didn't get more than eight or nine thousand dollars for the whole job; according to the cost sheets for the movie, the screenplay cost was $34,195.24, which wasn't much, even for that day, and the figure probably includes the salary and expenses of John Houseman and the others at Victorville. Mankiewicz may easily have felt he deserved an extra ten thousand. 'An Irish bum,' Johnson calls him – and if that makes him sound lovable, the operative word is still 'bum.' If Mankiewicz made up the story he told Johnson – and he was probably capable of such juicy slander – this kind of invention may be a clue to why Welles tries to turn the credit into blame. And if Mankiewicz did get the offer, did take the money, and did double-cross Welles, this might equally well explain why Welles doesn't want Mankiewicz to get any honor.

But Welles needed Mankiewicz. Since sound came in, almost every time an actor has scored in a role and become a 'star,' it has been because the role provided a realistic base for contradictory elements. Welles has never been able to write this kind of vehicle for himself. *Kane* may be a study of egotism and a movie about money and love, but it isn't just another movie about a rich man who isn't loved; it's a scandalously unauthorized, muckraking biography of a man who was still alive and – though past his peak influence – still powerful, so it conveyed shock and danger, and it drew its strength from its reverberations in the life of the period. Mankiewicz brought to the film the force of journalism. The thirties had been full of movie biographies of tycoons and robber barons, and some, like *The Power and the Glory*, were complexly told, but even Preston Sturges, as if in awe of the material, had taken a solemn, almost lachrymose approach to the money-doesn't-bring-happiness theme. Mankiewicz did it better: the prismatic technique turned into a masterly juggling act. There's an almost palpable sense of enjoyment in the script itself; Mankiewicz was skillful at making his points through comedy, and frequently it's higher, blacker comedy than was customary in the thirties pictures. Welles is a different kind of writer – theatrical and Gothic, not journalistic, and not *organized*. His later thrillers are portentous without having anything to portend, sensational in a void, entertaining thrillers, often, but *mere* thrillers.

Lacking the realistic base and the beautifully engineered structure that Mankiewicz provided, Welles has never again been able to release that charming, wicked rapport with the audience that he brought to *Kane* both as actor and as director (or has been able to release it only in distorted form, in self-satire and self-humiliation). He has brought many qualities to film – and there was perhaps a new, mellowed vitality in his work in the flawed *Falstaff* of a few years ago – but he has brought no more great original characters. In his movies, he can create an atmosphere but not a base. And without that the spirit that makes Kane so likable a bastard is missing. Kane, that mass of living contradictions, was conceived by Mankiewicz, an atheist who was proud of his kosher home, a man who was ambivalent about *both* Hearst and Welles.

However, things that get printed often enough begin to seep

into the general consciousness of the past, so there is a widespread impression that Welles wrote *Citizen Kane*. And even if one hadn't heard that he wrote it, and despite the presence in the film of so many elements and interests that are unrelated to Welles' other work (mundane activities and social content are not his forte), Kane and Welles are identified in our minds. This is not only a tribute to Welles as an actor but a backhanded tribute to Mankiewicz, who wrote the role for Welles the actor and wrote Welles the capricious, talented, domineering prodigy into the role, combining Welles' personality and character traits with Hearst's life in publishing and politics and acquisition.

If one asks how it is that Herman J. Mankiewicz, who wrote the film that many people think is the greatest film they've ever seen, is almost unknown, the answer must surely be not just that he died too soon but that he outsmarted himself. As a result of his wicked sense of humor in drawing upon Welles' character for Kane's, his own authorship was obscured. Sensing the unity of Kane and Welles, audiences assume that Kane is Welles' creation, that Welles is playing 'the role he was born to play,' while film scholars, seeing the material from Welles' life in the movie, interpret the film as Welles working out autobiographical themes. It is a commonplace in theatre talk to say that Olivier *is* Archie Rice or Olivier *is* Macbeth without assuming that the actor has conceived the role, but in movies we don't see other actors in the same role (except in remakes, which are usually very different in style), and film is so vivid and the actor so large and so close that it is a common primitive response to assume that the actor invented his lines. In this case, the primitive response is combined with the circumstances that Welles' name had been heavily featured for years, that the role was a new creation, that the movie audience's image of Welles was set by this overpowering role, in which they saw him for the first time, and that not only was the role partly based on him but he began to live up to it. Herman Mankiewicz died, and his share faded from knowledge, but Welles carries on in a baronial style that always reminds us of Kane. Kane seems an emanation of Welles, and if Mankiewicz didn't take the ten thousand, he might just as well have, because he helped stamp Welles all over the film.

19

James Agee, who didn't begin reviewing until later in 1941, wrote several years afterward that Welles had been 'fatuously overrated as a "genius",' and that he himself, annoyed by all the talk, had for a while underrated him. At the time the film was released, the most perceptive movie critic in the United States was Otis Ferguson (an early volunteer and early casualty in the Second World War), on the *New Republic*. Ferguson saw more clearly than anybody else what was specifically good and bad in *Kane*, and though he was wrong, I think, in maintaining that unobtrusive technique is the only good technique, he did perceive that *Citizen Kane* challenged this concept.

One of the games that film students sometimes play is to judge a director on whether you have the illusion that the people on the screen will go on doing what they're doing after the camera leaves them. Directors are rated by how much time you think elapsed before the actors grabbed their coats or ordered a sandwich. The longer the time, the more of a film man the director is said to be; when a director is stage-oriented, you can practically see the actors walking off the set. This game doesn't help in judging a film's content, but it's a fairly reliable test of a director's film technique; one could call it a test of movie believability. However, it isn't applicable to *Citizen Kane*. You're perfectly well aware that the people won't go on doing what they're doing – that they have, indeed, completed their actions on the screen. *Kane* depends not on naturalistic believability but on our enjoyment of the very fact that those actions *are* completed, and that they all fit into place. This bravura is, I think, the picture's only true originality, and it wasn't an intentional challenge to the concept of unobtrusive technique but was (mainly) the result of Welles' discovery of – and his delight in – the fun of making movies.

The best American directors in the thirties had been developing an unpretentious American naturalism; modern subjects and the advent of sound had freed them from the heavy dead hand of Germanic stage lighting and design. And so Ferguson was dismayed to see this all come back, and it *was* depressing that the critics who had always fallen for the synthetic serious were bowing and scraping and calling the picture 'deep' and 'realistic.' Probably so many people called it realistic because the social satire made contact with what they felt about Hearst and the country; when they used the term, they were referring to the content rather than the style. But it was the 'retrogressive' style that upset Ferguson – because it was when Orson Welles, an 'artist' director, joined the toughness and cynicism and the verbal skills of the thirties to that incomparable, faintly absurd, wonderfully overblown style of his that people said 'art.' Where Ferguson went wrong was in not recognizing one crucial element: that the unconcealed – even flaunted – pleasure that Welles took in all that claptrap made it new.

And it has kept it new. Even a number of those who worked on *Kane*, such as Houseman and Dorothy Comingore, have observed that the film seems to improve with the years. At the time, I got more simple, frivolous pleasure from Preston Sturges's *The Lady Eve*, which had come out a few months earlier, and I found more excitement in John Huston's *The Maltese Falcon*, which came out a few months later. At the time (I was twenty-one), I enjoyed *Kane* for the performances and the wit, but I was very conscious of how shallow the iconoclasm was. I don't think I was wrong, exactly, but now the movie seems marvellous to me. It's an *exuberant* shallow iconoclasm, and that youthful zest for shock and for the Expressionist theatricality seems to transform the shallowness. Now the movie sums up and preserves a period, and the youthful iconoclasm is preserved in all its freshness – even the freshness of its callowness. Now that the political theme (in its specific form, that is) is part of the past, the naïveté and obviousness fade, and what remains is a great American archetype and a popular legend – and so it has a strength that makes the artificially created comic world of a movie like *The Lady Eve* disappear by comparison. *Citizen Kane* has such energy it drives the viewer along. Though Mankiewicz provided the basic apparatus for it, that magical exuberance which fused the whole scandalous enterprise was Welles'. Works of art are enjoyed for different reasons in different periods; it may even be one of the defining characteristics of a lasting work of art that it yields up different qualities for admiration at different times. Welles' 'magic,' his extraordinary pleasure in playacting and illusion and in impressing an audience – what seems so charming about the movie now – was what seemed silly to me then. It was bouncy Pop Gothic in a period when the term 'comic strip' applied to works of art was still a term of abuse. Now Welles' discovery of movie-making – and the boyishness and excitement of that discovery – is preserved in *Kane* the way the snow scene is preserved in the glass ball.

Seeing the movie again recently, I liked the way it looked; now that the style no longer boded a return to the aestheticism of sets and the rigidly arranged figures of the German silents, I could enjoy it without misgivings. In the thirties, Jean Renoir had been using deep focus (that is, keeping the middle range and the background as clear as the foreground) in a naturalistic way. The light seemed (and often was) 'natural.' You looked at a scene, and the drama that you saw going on in it was just part of that scene, and so you had the sense of discovering it for yourself, of seeing drama in the midst of life. This was a tremendous relief from the usual studio lighting, which forced your attention to the dramatic action in the frame, blurred the rest, and rarely gave you a chance to feel that the action was part of anything larger or anything continuous. In Welles' far more extreme use of deep focus, and in his arrangement of the actors in the compositions, he swung back to the most coercive use of artificial, theatrical lighting. He used light like a spotlight on the stage, darkening or blacking out the irrelevant. He used deep focus not for a naturalistic effect but for the startling dramatic effect of having crucial action going on in the background (as when Kane appears in a distant doorway). The difference between Renoir's style and Welles' style seems almost literally the difference between day and night. Welles didn't have (nor did he, at that time, need) the kind of freedom Renoir needed and couldn't get in Hollywood – the freedom to shoot outside the studio and to depart from the script and improvise. *Kane* is a studio-made film – much of it was shot in that large room at R.K.O. where, a few years earlier, Ginger Rogers and Fred Astaire had danced their big numbers. However, Welles had the freedom to try out new solutions to technical problems, and he made his theatrical technique work spectacularly. Probably it was the first time in American movies that Expressionism had ever worked for comic and satiric effects (except in bits of some of the early spoof horror films), and probably it would have been impossible to tell the *Kane* story another way without spending a fortune on crowds and set construction. Welles' method is a triumph of ingenuity in that the pinpoints of light in the darkness conceal the absence of detailed sets (a chair or two and a huge fireplace, and one thinks one is seeing a great room), and the almost treacherously brilliant use of sound conceals the absence of crowds. We see Susan at the *deserted* cabaret; we see her from the back on the opera-house stage and we imagine that she is facing an audience; we get a sense of crowds at the political rally without seeing them. It was Welles' experience both in the theatre and in radio that enabled him to produce a huge historical film on a shoestring; he produced the *illusion* of a huge historical film.

But, seeing *Kane* now, I winced, as I did the first time, at the empty virtuosity of the shot near the beginning when Kane, dying, drops the glass ball and we see the nurse's entrance reflected in the glass. I noticed once again, though without being bothered by it this time, either, that there was no one in the room to hear the dying Kane say 'Rosebud.' I was much more disturbed by little picky defects, like the obtrusive shot up to the bridge before the reporter goes into the hospital. What is strange about reseeing a movie that one reacted to fairly intensely many years ago is that one may respond exactly the same way to so many details and *be aware* each time of having responded that way before. I was disappointed once again by the clumsily staged 'cute' meeting of Kane and Susan, which seemed to belong to a routine comedy, and I thought the early scenes with Susan were weak not just because while listening to her dull, sentimental singing Welles is in a passive position and so can't animate the scenes but – and mainly – because the man of simple pleasures who would find a dumb girl deeply appealing does not tie in with the personality projected by Orson Welles. (And as Welles doesn't project any sexual interest in either Kane's first wife, Emily, or in Susan, his second wife, we don't know how to interpret Susan's claim that he just likes her voice.) Most of the newspaper-office scenes looked as clumsily staged as ever, and the first appearance of Bernstein, Kane's business manager, arriving with a load of furniture, was still confusing. (He seems to be a junk dealer – probably because an earlier scene in *American* introducing him was eliminated.) I disliked again the attempt to wring humor out of the sputtering confusion of Carter, the old Dickensian editor. It's a scene like the ones Mankiewicz helped prepare for the Marx Brothers, but what was probably intended to make fun of a stuffed shirt turned into making fun of a helpless old man trying to keep his dignity, which is mean and barbarous. I still thought Susan became too thin a conception, and more shrill and shrewish than necessary, and, as Emily, Ruth Warrick was all pursed lips – a stereotype of refinement. I was still uncomfortable during the visit to Jed Leland in the hospital; Leland's character throughout is dependent on Joseph Cotten's obvious charm, and the sentimental-old-codger bit in this sequence is really a disgrace. The sequence plays all too well at a low conventional level – pulling out easy stops. I still didn't see the function of the sequence about Kane's being broke and losing control of his empire, since nothing followed from it. (I subsequently discovered that things weren't going well on the set at one point, and Welles decided to go back to this scene, which had been in an earlier draft and had then been eliminated. What it coördinated with was, unfortunately, not restored.) This sequence also has the most grating bad line in the movie, when Kane says, 'You know, Mr Bernstein, if I hadn't been very rich, I might have been a really great man.'

What's still surprising is how well a novice movie director handled so many of the standard thirties tricks and caricatures – the device of the alternative newspaper headlines, for example, and the stock explosive, hand-waving Italian opera coach (well played by Fortunio Bonanova). The engineering – the way the sequences are prepared for and commented on by preceding sequences, the way the five accounts tie together to tell the story – seems as ingenious as ever; though one is aware that the narrators are telling things they couldn't have witnessed, one accepts this as part of the convention. The cutting (which a reading of the script reveals to have been carried out almost exactly as it was planned) is elegantly precise, and some sequences have a good, sophomoric musical-comedy buoyancy.

What had changed for me – what I had once enjoyed but now found almost mysteriously *beautiful* – was Orson Welles' performance. An additional quality that old movies acquire is that people can be seen as they once were. It is a pleasure we can't get in theatre; we can only hear and read descriptions of past fabulous performances. But here in *Kane* is the young Welles, and he seems almost embarrassed to be exposed as so young. Perhaps he *was* embarrassed, and that's why he so often hid in extravagant roles and behind those old-man false faces. He seems unsure of himself as the young Kane, and there's something very engaging (and surprisingly *human*) about Welles unsure of himself; he's a big, overgrown, heavy boy, and rather sheepish, one suspects, at being seen as he is. Many years later, Welles remarked, 'Like most performers, I naturally prefer a live audience to that lie-detector full of celluloid.' Maybe his spoiled-baby face was just too nearly perfect for the role, and he knew it, and knew the hostile humor that lay behind Mankiewicz's putting so much of him in the role of Hearst the braggart self-publicist and making Kane so infantile. That statement of principles that Jed sends back to Kane and that Kane then tears up must surely refer to the principles behind the co-founding of the Mercury Theatre by Welles and Houseman. Lines like Susan's 'You're not a professional magician, are you?' may have made Welles flinch. And it wasn't just the writer who played games on him. There's the scene of Welles eating in the newspaper office, which was obviously caught by the camera crew, and which, to be 'a good sport,' he had to use. Welles is one of the most self-conscious of actors – it's part of his rapport with the audience – and this is what is so nakedly revealed in this role, in which he's playing a young man his own age and he's insecure (and with some reason) about what's coming through. Something of the young, unmasked man is revealed in these scenes – to be closed off forever after.

Welles picks up assurance and flair as Kane in his thirties, and he's also good when Kane is just a little older and jowly. I think there's no doubt that he's more sure of himself when he's playing this somewhat older Kane, and this is the Kane we remember best from the first viewing – the brash, confident Kane of the pre-election-disaster period. He's so fully – classically – American a showoff one almost regrets the change of title. But when I saw the movie again it was the younger Kane who stayed with me – as if I had been looking through a photograph album and had come upon a group of pictures of an old friend, long dead, as he had been when I first met him. I had almost forgotten Welles in his youth, and here he is, smiling, eager, looking forward to the magnificent career that everyone expected him to have.

20

Just as Welles suggested the radio-bulletin approach to the H. G. Wells landing-of-the-Martians material to Howard Koch, he may very well have suggested the 'March of Time' summary of Hearst's career in his early talks with Mankiewicz. Welles had worked as an actor for the 'March of Time' radio program in 1934 and 1935, and he had worked steadily as a narrator and radio actor (his most famous role was the lead in the popular weekly mystery show 'The Shadow') until he went to Hollywood. The 'March of Time' is exactly the kind of idea the young Welles *would* have suggested. It's the sort of technique that was being used in the experimental theatre of the late thirties – when the Federal Theatre Project (in which Welles and Houseman had worked together) staged the documentary series 'The Living Newspaper,' and when members of the Group Theatre and other actors were performing anti-Fascist political cabaret. The imitation 'March of Time' was not a new device, even in movies; it had already been used, though humorlessly, to convey the fact that a theme was current, part of 'today's news,' and to provide background information – as in *Confessions of a Nazi Spy*, of 1939. What was needed to transform that device and make it the basis for the memorable parody in *Citizen Kane* was not only Welles' experience and not only his 'touch' but the great sense of mischief that he and Mankiewicz shared. The smug manner of the 'March of Time' was already a joke to many people; when I was a student at Berkeley in the late thirties, there was always laughter in the theatres when the 'March of Time' came on, with its racy neo-conservatism and its ritual pomposity – with that impersonal tone, as if God above were narrating. There was an element of unconscious self-parody in the important tone of the 'March of Time,' as in all the Luce enterprises, and, in his script, Mankiewicz pushed it further. He used consciously those elements which part of the public already found funny, bringing into a mass medium what was already a subject for satire among the knowledge-able.

Mankiewicz's 'On Approaching Forty' had not appeared in *The New Yorker*, but a few weeks after it was printed, in 1936, Wolcott Gibbs, who was to take Mankiewicz's old chair as *The New Yorker*'s drama critic (and who was the first occupant of that chair not to emigrate to Hollywood), published the celebrated Profile 'Time – Fortune – Life – Luce,' which was written in mock Timese ('Backward ran sentences until reeled the mind,' and so on, concluding with 'Where it all will end, knows God!'), and this was probably not merely the spur to Mankiewicz but the competition. Mankiewicz's pastiche was fully worked out in the first long draft of the script, the processed prose and epigrams already honed to perfection ('For forty years appeared in Kane newsprint no public issue on which Kane papers took no stand. No public man whom Kane himself did not support or denounce – often support, then denounce'). And even on paper – without Welles' realization of the plan – the section is good enough to invite the comparison that I suspect Mankiewicz sought with the Gibbs parody. (Mankiewicz's widow keeps the Oscar statuette for *Citizen Kane* on the mantel, along with the latest *Who's Who in America* with the marker set at her sons' listings, and on the shelf next to the mantel are the bound volumes of *The New Yorker* in which her husband's reviews appeared.)

Part of the fun of the 'March of Time' parody for the audiences back in 1941 was that, of course, we kept *recognizing* things about Hearst in it, and its daring meant great suspense about what was to follow in the picture. But Mankiewicz tried to do more with this parody than is completely evident either in the final script or in the film itself. He tried to use the 'March of Time' as a historical framing device to close one era and open the next, with Hearstian journalism giving way to the new Luce empire. In the movie, it seems a structural gimmick – though a very cleverly *used* gimmick, which is enjoyable in itself. In Mankiewicz's original conception, in the long first-draft *American*, which ran three hundred and twenty-five pages, that device is more clearly integral to the theme. In Mankiewicz's conception, the Hearst-Kane empire is doomed: Kane's own death is being 'sent' to the world by the filmed 'March of Time' (called 'News on the March' in the movie), which means the end of the newspaper business as Hearst knew it. The funny thing is that Mankiewicz, in commenting on Hearst's lack of vision, overestimated Luce's vision. After Luce took news coverage from newspapers into newsmagazines, he moved into photo-journalism and then into news documentaries, but he didn't follow through on what he had started, and he failed to get into television production. Now, after *his* death, the Luce organization is trying to get back into film activities.

In Mankiewicz's original conception, the historical line of succession was laid out as in a chronicle play. Hearst supplanted the old-style quiet upper-class journalism with his penny-dreadful treatment of crime and sex and disasters, his attacks on the rich, his phony lawsuits against the big corporations that he called 'predators,' his screaming patrio-tism, his faked photographs, and his exploitation of supersti-tion, plus puzzles, comics, contests, sheet music, and medical quackery. His youthful dedication to the cause of the common people declined into the cheap chauvinism that infected everything and helped to turn the readers into a political mob. The irony built into the structure was that his own demise should be treated in the new, lofty style of Luce.

And it was in terms of this framework that the elements of admiration in the ambivalent portrait of Kane made sense. Hearst represented a colorful kind of journalism that was already going out. Mankiewicz was summing up the era of *The Front Page* at the end of it, and was treating it right at its source in the American system that made it possible for a rich boy to inherit the power to control public opinion as his own personal plaything. *American* (and, to a lesser degree, *Citizen Kane*) was a there-were-giants-in-those-days valedictory to the old-style big scoundrels. The word had been used straight by Mrs Fremont Older in 1936 when she published the authorized biography, *William Randolph Hearst, American*. 'American' was Hearst's shibboleth; his Sunday magazine section was the *American Weekly*, and he had been changing his newspaper titles to include the word 'American' whenever possible ever since Senator Henry Cabot Lodge accused him of being un-American in those days after the McKinley assassination when Hearst was hanged in effigy. Hearst's attacks on McKinley as 'the most despised and hated creature in the hemisphere' had culminated in an editorial that said 'Killing must be done' shortly before it was. When the storm died down, Hearst became super-American. For Mankiewicz, Hearst's Americanism was the refuge of a scoundrel, though by no means his last refuge; *that*, in the first draft, was clearly blackmail. What the title was meant to signify was indicated by Kane in the 'News on the March' segment when he said, 'I am, have been, and will be only one thing – an American.' That was pure flag-waving Pop before we had a name for it: 'American' as it was used by the American Legion and the Daughters of the American Revolution. In addition, Mankiewicz may have wanted to score off his movie friends who since the middle thirties – the period of the Popular Front – had also been draping themselves in the flag. In that period, the Communist left had become insistent about its American-ism, in its rather embarrassing effort to tout American democracy, which it had called 'imperialism' until the U.S.S.R. sought the United States as an ally against Hitler. In the later title, 'Citizen' is similarly ironic; Hearst, the offspring of an economic baron, and himself a press lord and the master of San Simeon, was a 'citizen' the way Louis XIV at Versailles was a citizen. And joining the word to 'Kane' (Cain) made its own point.

Both the parodistic use of Timese and the facelessness of Luce's company men served a historical purpose in the first script. But *American* was much too long and inclusive and loose, and much too ambitious, and Mankiewicz rapidly cut it down (copies of these gradually shorter drafts were saved) until it reached the hundred and fifty-six pages of the final shooting script – which still made for a then unusually long picture, of a hundred and nineteen minutes. In the trimming, dialogue that was crucial to the original dramatic conception of the Hearst-Luce succession was cut. (In terms of the final conception, though, it's perfectly clear why.) This deleted exchange between Thompson, the investigating reporter for the Rawlston (Luce) organization, and Raymond, Kane's butler, makes the point about the line of succession from Hearst to Luce all too explicity:

THOMPSON

Well, if you get around to your memoirs – don't forget, Mr Rawlston wants to be sure of getting first chance. We pay awful well for long excerpts.

RAYMOND

Maybe he'd like to buy the excerpts of what Mr Kane said about him.

THOMPSON
Huh?

RAYMOND

He thought Rawlston would break his neck sooner or later. He gave that weekly magazine of yours three years.

THOMPSON
(*Smugly*) He made a bit of a mistake.

RAYMOND
He made a lot of mistakes.

Welles, who did such memorable casting in the rest of the movie, used a number of his own faceless executive assistants in the vapid roles of the Luce men. They are the performers in *Citizen Kane* that nobody remembers, and they didn't go on to become actors. William Alland, whose voice was fine as the voice of 'News on the March' but who was a vacuum as Thompson, the reporter, became a producer and investment broker; another of Welles' assistants, Richard Wilson, who also played a reporter, is now a director (*Three in the Attic*); still another, Richard Barr, is the well-known New York theatrical producer. Among the 'News on the March' men, there were some bit players who did have potential faces (Alan Ladd was one of them), but they weren't presented as personalities. Nevertheless, in a movie as verbally explicit as *Citizen Kane* the faceless idea doesn't really come across. You probably don't get the intention behind it in *Kane* unless you start thinking about the unusual feebleness of the scenes with the 'News on the March' people and about the fact that though Thompson is a principal in the movie in terms of how much he appears, there isn't a shred of characterization in his lines or in his performance; he is such a shadowy presence that you may even have a hard time remembering whether you ever saw his face, though this movie introduced to the screen a large group of performers who made strong, astonishingly distinct impressions, sometimes in very brief roles. Perhaps the acting and the group movement of the faceless men needed to be more stylized, the dialogue more satirical; as it was done, it's just dull rather than purposefully blank. Welles probably thought it didn't matter how bad these actors were, because they should be colorless anyway; after R.K.O. gave him the go-ahead on the project, he didn't reshoot the test scene he had made of the projection-room sequence. But the movie misses on the attitudes *behind* Luce's new journalism. It's true that for the practitioners of Timese impersonality becomes their personal style and reporters become bureaucrats, but there's also a particular aura of programmed self-importance and of awareness of power – the ambitiousness of colorless people.

Among the minor absurdities of the script is that the 'News on the March' men never think of sending a cameraman along with the inquiring reporter, though Gable had just played a newsreel cameraman in *Too Hot to Handle*, in 1938, and though in *The Philadelphia Story*, which had opened on Broadway in 1939, and which Mankiewicz's brother Joe produced for the screen in 1940, while *Kane* was being shot, the magazine team, also obviously from Luce, includes a photographer. There's something rather pathetic – almost as if *Kane* were a Grade B movie that didn't have a big enough budget for a few extra players – about that one lonely sleuthing reporter travelling around the country while a big organization delays the release of an important newsreel documentary on the head of a rival news chain. Maybe Mankiewicz, despite his attempt to place Hearst historically through the 'March of Time' framework, still thought in terms of the older journalism and of all the gimmicky movies about detective-reporters. And Mankiewicz was by temperament a reckless, colorful newspaperman. That deleted material about the Luce organization's wanting Raymond's memoirs, with Raymond's teaser 'He made a lot of mistakes,' is part of an elaborate series of scandalous subplots, closely paralleling scandals in Hearst's life, that were cut out in the final script. In the movie, Susan says to Thompson, 'Look, if you're smart, you'll get in touch with Raymond. He's the butler. You'll learn a lot from him. He knows where all the bodies are buried.' It's an odd, cryptic speech. In the first draft, Raymond *literally* knew where the bodies were buried: Mankiewicz had dished up a nasty version of the scandal sometimes referred to as the Strange Death of Thomas Ince. Even with this kind of material cut down to the barest allusions, Mankiewicz, in *Citizen Kane*, treated the material of Hearst's life in Hearstian yellow-journalism style.

21

Welles is right, of course, about Rosebud – it *is* dollar-book Freud. But it is such a primitive kind of Freudianism that, like some of the movie derivations from Freud later in the forties – in *The Seventh Veil*, for instance – it hardly seems Freudian at all now. Looking for 'the secret' of a famous man's last words is about as phony as the blind-beggar-for-luck bit, yet it does 'work' for some people; they go for the idea that Rosbud represents lost maternal bliss and somehow symbolizes Kane's loss of the power to love or be loved. The one significant change from Hearst's life – Kane's separation from his parents – seems to be used to explain Kane, though there is an explicit disavowal of any such intention toward the end. Someone says to Thompson, 'If you could have found out what Rosebud meant, I bet that would've explained everything.' Thompson replies, 'No, I don't think so. No. Mr Kane was a man who got everything he wanted, and then lost it. Maybe Rosebud was something he couldn't get or something he lost. Anyway, it wouldn't have explained anything. I don't think any word can explain a man's life. No. I guess Rosebud is just a piece in a jigsaw puzzle, a missing piece.'

Nevertheless, the structure of the picture – searching for the solution to a mystery – and the exaggerated style make it appear that Rosebud *is* the key to Kane's life, and the public responds to what is presented dramatically, not to the reservations of the moviemakers. Rosebud has become part of popular culture, and people remember it who have forgotten just about everything else in *Citizen Kane*; the jokes started a week before the movie opened, with a child's sled marked 'Rosebud' dragged onstage in the first act of *Native Son*, and a couple of years ago, in *Peanuts*, Snoopy walked in the snow pulling a sled and Charlie Brown said, 'Rosebud?' The Rosebud of Rosebud is as banal as Rosebud itself. It seems that as a child Herman Mankiewicz had had a sled, which may or may not have carried the label 'Rosebud' (his family doesn't remember); he wasn't dramatically parted from the sled, but he once had a bicycle that was stolen, and he mourned that all his life. He simply put the emotion of the one onto the other.

Though Rosebud was in the long first draft, it didn't carry the same weight there, because the newspaper business itself undermined Kane's idealism. In that draft, Kane, like Hearst, in order to reach the masses he thought he wanted to serve and protect, built circulation by turning the newspapers into pulp magazines, and, in order to stay in business and expand, squeezed non-advertisers. The long script went as far as to show that, in the process of becoming one of the mighty, Kane-Hearst, like Louis B. Mayer and so many other tycoons, developed close ties to the underworld. Mankiewicz was trying to give a comprehensive view of the contradictions that emerge when an idealist attempts to succeed in business and politics. Fragments of this are left, but their meaning is no longer clear. For example, the point of the sequence of Kane's buying up the staff of the *Chronicle*, the paper that was outselling his *Inquirer* by featuring crime and sex, was that the *Chronicle*'s staff would change him by deflecting him from an idealist course (and Jed tries to point this out to Bernstein), but as it appears in the film it almost seems that in buying the *Chronicle*'s staff Kane is corrupting *them*.

It is just a fragment, too, that Kane's first wife, Emily, is the niece of the President of the United States. Hearst's only wife, Millicent, the daughter of a vaudeville hoofer, was a teen-age member of a group called The Merry Maidens when he met her. Emily was probably made the niece of the President in order to link Kane with the rich and to make a breach in the marriage when Kane was held responsible for the assassination of the President (as Hearst was accused of having incited the death of President McKinley).

In the condensation, the whole direction was, for commercial reasons, away from the newspaper business that dominated the early script, and, for obvious reasons, away from factual resemblances to Hearst's life. This was generally accomplished by making things funny. For example, Hearst had actually been cheated out of the office of mayor of New York by fraud at the polls, and this incident was included in *American*. In *Citizen Kane* it became, instead, a joke: when Kane loses the election for governor, the Kane papers automatically claim 'FRAUD AT POLLS.' This version is, of course, a quick way of dramatizing the spirit of yellow journalism, and it's useful and comic, but the tendency of this change, as of many others, was, whether deliberately or unconsciously, to make things easier for the audience by playing down material on how wealth and the power it buys can also buy the love of the voters. Hearst (the son of a senator whose money had got him into the Senate) did buy his way into public office; as a young man, he was twice elected to Congress, and he had tried to get the Democratic nomination for President just before he decided to run for mayor of New York. The movie flatters the audience by saying that Kane couldn't buy the people's love – that he 'was never granted elective office by the voters of his country.'

Actually, it wasn't the voters but crooked politicians who defeated Hearst. When the Tammany boss Charles F. Murphy refused to help Hearst get the Democratic nomination for mayor, he ran as an independent, campaigning against the corrupt Tammany 'boodlers,' and he printed a cartoon of Murphy in prison stripes. Kane gives Boss Jim Gettys this treatment. Murphy was so deeply wounded by the cartoon that he arranged for Hearst's ballots to be stolen, and, it is said, even managed to rig the recount. That reckless cartoon was the turning point in Hearst's political career. The movie gives Gettys a different revenge; namely, exposing Kane's 'love nest'

– which was something that also happened to Hearst, but on another occasion, long after he had abandoned his political ambitions, when his *Los Angeles Examiner* was attacking the *Los Angeles Times*, and the *Times* used his own tactics against him by bringing up his 'double life' and his 'love nest' with Marion Davies. The movie ultimately plays the same game. *Citizen Kane* becomes a movie about the private life of a public figure – the scandals and tidbits and splashy sensations that the Hearst press always preferred to issues. The assumption of the movie was much like that of the yellow press: that the mass audience wasn't interested in issues, that all it wanted was to get 'behind the scenes' and find out the dirt.

22

As the newspaper business and the political maneuvering were pared away, the personal material took on the weight and the shape of the solution to a mystery. Even so, if the movie had been directed in a more matter-of-fact, naturalistic style, Thompson's explanation that Rosebud was just a piece in a jigsaw puzzle would have seemed quite sensible. Instead, Welles' heavily theatrical style overemphasized the psychological explanation to such a point that when we finally glimpse the name on the sled we in the audience are made to feel that we're in on a big secret – a revelation that the world missed out on. However, Rosebud is so cleverly worked into the structure that, like the entrance that Hecht and MacArthur prepared for Walter Burns, it is enjoyable as beautiful tomfoolery even while we are conscious of it as 'commercial' mechanics. I think what makes Welles' directional style so satisfying in this movie is that we are constantly aware of the mechanics – that the pleasure *Kane* gives doesn't come from illusion but comes from our enjoyment of the dexterity of the illusionists and the working of the machinery. *Kane*, too, is a clock that laughs. *Citizen Kane* is a film made by a very young man of enormous spirit; he took the Mankiewicz material and he played with it, he turned it into a magic show. It is Welles' distinctive quality as a movie director – I think it is his genius – that he never hides his cleverness, that he makes it possible for us not only to enjoy what he does but to share his enjoyment in doing it. Welles' showmanship is right there on the surface, just as it was when, as a stage director, he set *Julius Caesar* among the Nazis, and set *Macbeth* in Haiti with a black cast and, during the banquet scene, blasted the audience with a recording of the 'Blue Danube Waltz' – an effect that Kubrick was to echo (perhaps unknowingly?) in *2001*. There is something childlike – and great, too – about his pleasure in the magic of theatre and movies. No other director in the history of movies has been so open in his delight, so eager to share with us the game of pretending, and Welles' silly pretense of having done everything himself is just another part of the game.

Welles' magic as a director (at this time) was that he could put his finger right on the dramatic fun of each scene. Mankiewicz had built the scenes to end at ironic, dramatic high points, and Welles probably had a more innocently brazen sense of melodramatic timing than any other movie director. Welles also had a special magic beyond this: he could give *élan* to scenes that were confused in intention, so that the movie seems to go from dramatic highlight to highlight without lagging in between. There doesn't appear to be any waste material in *Kane*, because he charges right through the weak spots as if they were bright, and he almost convinces you (or *does* convince you) that they're shining jewels. Perhaps these different kinds of magic can be suggested by two examples. There's the famous sequence in which Kane's first marriage is summarized by a series of breakfasts, with overlapping dialogue. The method was not new, and it's used here on a standard marriage joke, but the joke is a basic good joke, and the method is honestly used to sum up as speedily as possible the banality of what goes wrong with the marriage. This sequence is adroit, and Welles brings out the fun in the material, but there's no *special* Wellesian magic in it – except, perhaps, in his own acting. But in the cutting from the sequence of Kane's first meeting with Susan (where the writing supplies almost no clue to why he's drawn to this particular twerp of a girl beyond his finding her relaxing) to the political rally, Welles' special talent comes into play. Welles directs the individual scenes with such flourish and such *enjoyment of flourish* that the audience reacts as if the leap into the rally were clever and funny and logical, too, although the connection between the scenes isn't established until later, when Boss Jim Gettys uses Susan to wreck Kane's political career. As a director, Welles is so ebullient that we go along with the way he wants us to feel; we're happy to let him 'put it over on us.' Given the subject of Hearst and the witty script, the effect is of complicity, of a shared knowingness between Welles and the audience about what the movie is about. Kane's big smile at the rally seals the pact between him and us. Until Kane's later years, Welles, in the role, has an almost total empathy with the audience. It's the same kind of empathy we're likely to feel for smart kids who grin at us when they're showing off in the school play. It's a beautiful kind of emotional nakedness – ingenuously exposing the sheer love of playacting – that most actors lose long before they become 'professional.' If an older actor – even a very good one – had played the role, faking youth for the young Kane the way Edward Arnold, say, sometimes faked it, I think the picture might have been routine. Some people used to say that Welles might be a great director but he was a bad actor, and his performances wrecked his pictures. I think just the opposite – that his directing style is such an emanation of his adolescent love of theatre that his films lack a vital unifying element when he's not in them or when he plays only a small part in them. He needs to be at the center. *The*

Magnificent Ambersons is a work of feeling and imagination and of obvious effort – and the milieu is much closer to Welles' own background than the milieu of *Kane* is – but Welles isn't in it, and it's too bland. It feels empty, uninhabited. Without Orson Welles' physical presence – the pudgy, big prodigy, who incarnates egotism – *Citizen Kane* might (as Otis Ferguson suggested) have disintegrated into vignettes. We feel that he's making it all happen. Like the actor-managers of the old theatre, he's the man onstage running the show, pulling it all together.

23

Mankiewicz's script, though nominally an 'original' – and in the best sense original – was in large part an adaptation of the material (much of it published) of Hearst's life. Hearst's life was so full of knavery and perversity that Mankiewicz simply sorted out the plums. Mankiewicz had been a reporter on the *New York World*, the Pulitzer paper, where Hearst himself had worked for a time before he persuaded his father to give him the *San Francisco Examiner*. When Hearst got the *Examiner*, he changed it in imitation of the *World*, and then expanded to New York, where he bought a paper and started raiding and decimating the *World*'s staff. One of his favorite tactics was to hire away men he didn't actually want at double or treble what Pulitzer was paying them, then fire them, leaving them stranded (a tactic memorialized in *The Front Page* when Walter Burns hires and fires the poetic reporter Bensinger). Kane's business practices are so closely patterned on Hearst's that in reading about Hearst one seems to be reading the script. Descriptions – like the one in the *Atlantic Monthly* in 1931 – of how Hearst cynically bought away the whole of Pulitzer's Sunday staff might be descriptions of Kane's maneuver. In 1935, *Fortune* described Hearst's warehouse in the Bronx in terms that might have been the specifications for the ware-house in the film, and by 1938 even the *Reader's Digest* was reprinting, from the *Saturday Evening Post*, a description of Hearst's empire in phrases that might be part of the script:

All his life Mr Hearst bought, bought, bought – whatever touched his fancy. He purchased newspapers, Egyptian mummies, a California mountain range, herds of Tibetan yaks. He picked up a Spanish abbey, had it knocked down, crated, shipped to New York, and never has seen it since.

To his shares in the Homestake, largest gold producer in the United States, his Peruvian copper mines, his 900,000 acre Mexican cattle ranch, and his other inherited proper-ties, he added 28 daily newspapers, 14 magazines here and in England, eight radio stations, wire services, a Hollywood producing unit, a newsreel, a castle in Wales, and one of the world's largest collections of objects d'art, gathered at a toll of $40,000,000.

Kane's dialogue is often almost Hearst verbatim; in the margin of the script that Mankiewicz lent to Charles Lederer one of Hearst's lawyers annotated Kane's speech beginning, 'Young man, there'll be no war. I have talked with the responsible leaders,' with the words 'This happens to be the gist of an authentic interview with WRH – occasion, his last trip from Europe.' Some of the dialogue was legendary long before the movie was made. When Hearst was spending a fortune in his circulation war with Pulitzer, someone told his mother that Willie was losing money at the rate of a million dollars a year, and she equably replied, 'Is he? Then he will only last about thirty years.' This is no more than slightly transposed in the film, though it's really milked:

THATCHER

Tell me, honestly, my boy, don't you think it's rather unwise

to continue this philanthropic enterprise . . . this 'Inquirer'
that is costing you a million dollars a year?

KANE

You're right, Mr Thatcher. I did lose a million dollars last
year. I expect to lose a million dollars this year. I expect to
lose a million dollars next year. You know, Mr Thatcher, at
the rate of a million dollars a year . . . I'll have to close this
place in sixty years.

(To audiences in 1941, Thatcher, appearing at the congres-
sional-committee hearing, was obviously J. P. Morgan the
younger, and the Thatcher Library was, of course, the
Pierpont Morgan Library.)

Mankiewicz could hardly improve on the most famous of all
Hearst stories, so he merely touched it up a trifle. According to
many accounts, Hearst, trying to foment war with Spain, had
sent Richard Harding Davis to Havana to write about the
Spanish atrocities and Frederic Remington to sketch them.
Remington grew restless there and sent Hearst a telegram:

EVERYTHING IS QUIET. THERE IS NO TROUBLE HERE.
THERE WILL BE NO WAR. I WISH TO RETURN. REMING-
TON.

Hearst replied,

PLEASE REMAIN. YOU FURNISH THE PICTURES AND I'LL
FURNISH THE WAR. W. R. HEARST.

In the movie, Bernstein reads Kane a telegram from a
reporter named Wheeler:

GIRLS DELIGHTFUL IN CUBA, STOP. COULD SEND YOU

PROSE POEMS ABOUT SCENERY BUT DON'T FEEL RIGHT
SPENDING YOUR MONEY, STOP. THERE IS NO WAR IN
CUBA. SIGNED WHEELER.

And Bernstein asks, 'Any answer?'
Kane replies:

DEAR WHEELER, YOU PROVIDE THE PROSE POEMS, I'LL
PROVIDE THE WAR.

These stories were so well known at the time of the movie's
release that in the picture spread on the movie in *Life* (with
captions in the very style that Mankiewicz had parodied in his
'News on the March') the magazine – unconsciously, no doubt
– returned to the Hearst original, and flubbed even that:

> Kane buys a newspaper in New York and sets out to be a
> great social reformer. But even at 25 he is unscrupulous
> and wangles the U.S. into war by fake news dispatches. To
> a cartoonist in Cuba he wires: 'You get the pictures and I'll
> make the war.'

One passage of dialogue that is bad because it sounds
slanted to make an ideological point is almost a straight steal
(and that's probably why Mankiewicz didn't realize how
fraudulent it would sound), and was especially familiar
because John Dos Passos had quoted it in *U.S.A.*, in his
section on Hearst, 'Poor Little Rich Boy.' (That title might be
the theme of the movie.) Dos Passos quotes Hearst's answer
to fellow-millionaires who thought he was a traitor to his class:

> You know I believe in property, and you know where I
> stand on personal fortunes, but isn't it better that I should

nt in this country the dissatisfied than have some-
~~~e do it who might not have the same real property
relations that I may have?

Hearst apparently did say it, but even though it's made
more conversational in the movie, it's unconvincing – it
sounds like left-wing paranoia.

KANE

I'll let you in on another little secret, Mr Thatcher. I think
I'm the man to do it. You see, I have money and property.
If I don't look after the interests of the underprivileged
maybe somebody else will . . . maybe somebody without
any money or property.

Despite the fake childhood events, Kane's life story follows
Hearst's much more closely than most movie biographies
follow acknowledged and named subjects. Kane is burned in
effigy, as Hearst was, and there is even a reference to Kane's
expulsion from Harvard; one of the best-known stories in
America was how young Willie Hearst had been expelled
from Harvard after sending each of his instructors a chamber
pot with the recipient's name handsomely lettered on the
inside bottom. Even many of the subsidiary characters are
replicas of Hearst's associates. For example, Bernstein (given
the name of Welles' old guardian) is obviously Solomon S.
Carvalho, the business manager of Pulitzer's *World*, whom
Hearst hired away, and who became the watchdog of the
Journal's exchequer and Hearst's devoted business manager.
There was no special significance in the use of Mankiewicz's
secretary's last name for Susan Alexander, or in naming Jed
Leland for Leland Hayward (Mankiewicz's agent, whose wife,
Margaret Sullavan, spent a weekend visiting at Victorville),
just as there was no significance in the fact that the actor

Whitford Kane had been part of the nucleus of the Mercu.
Theatre, but the use of the name Bernstein for Kane's
devoted, uncritical friend had some significance in relation not
only to Welles but to Hearst, and it was Mankiewicz's way of
giving Hearst points (he did it in the breakfast scene when
Emily is snobbish about Bernstein) because, whatever else
Hearst was, he was not a snob or an anti-Semite. (For one
thing, Marion's brother-in-law – Charles Lederer's father –
was Jewish.) No doubt Mankiewicz also meant to give Kane
points when he had him finish Jed's negative review of Susan's
singing in the same negative spirit – which was more than
George S. Kaufman had done for Mankiewicz's review back
at the *New York Times*. This episode is perversely entertaining
but not convincing. *Kane* used so much of Hearst's already
legendary life that for liberals it was like a new kind of folk art;
we knew all this about Hearst from books and magazines but
gasped when we saw it on the big movie screen, and so
defiantly – almost contemptuously – undisguised.

The departure from Hearst's life represented by Susan
Alexander's opera career, which is a composite of the loves
and scandals of several Chicago tycoons, didn't weaken the
attack on Hearst – it strengthened it. Attaching the other
scandals to him made him seem the epitome of the powerful
and spoiled, and thus stand for them all. Opera – which used
to be called 'grand opera' – was a ritual target of American
comedy. It was an easier target for the public to respond to
than Hearst's own folly – motion pictures – because the public
already connected opera with wealth and temperament,
tycoons in opera hats and women in jewels, imported prima
donnas, and all the affectations of 'culture.' It was a world the
movie public didn't share, and it was already absurd in
American movies – the way valets and effete English butlers
and the high-toned Americans putting on airs who kept them
were absurd. George S. Kaufman and Morrie Ryskind had

115

ra over in two of the Marx Brothers pictures; ad been taken off *A Night at the Opera*, but what welles – with the assistance of Bernard Herrmann – to opera in *Citizen Kane* was in almost exactly the same style, and as funny.

Mankiewicz was working overseas for the *Chicago Tribune* when Harold McCormick and his wife, Edith Rockefeller McCormick, were divorced, in 1921. The McCormicks had been the leading patrons of opera in Chicago; they had made up the Chicago Opera Company's deficits, which were awe-inspiring during the time the company was under the management of Mary Garden (she chose to be called the 'directa'), rising to a million dollars one great, lavish season. After the divorce, McCormick married Ganna Walska, the preëminent temperamental mediocre soprano of her day. Mankiewicz combined this scandal with a far more widely publicized event that occurred a few years later, replacing Hearst and Cosmopolitan Pictures with Samuel Insull and his building of the Chicago Civic Opera House. Insull didn't build the opera house for his wife (dainty little Gladys Wallis didn't sing), but there was a story to it, and it was the biggest opera story of the decade. After the McCormick-Rockefeller divorce, their joint largesse to opera ended, and the deficits were a big problem. Insull, 'the Czar of Commonwealth Edison,' who also loved opera (and dallied with divas), wanted to put it on a self-supporting business basis. He concluded that if an opera house should be built in a skyscraper, the rental of the upper regions would eventually cover the opera's deficits. The building was started in 1928; it had forty-five stories, with the opera company occupying the first six, and with Insull's office-lair on top. The structure was known as 'Insull's throne,' and it cost twenty million dollars. The opening of the new opera house was scheduled for November 4, 1929; six days before, on October 29th, the

stock market crashed. The opening took place du
panic, with plainclothesmen and eight detective-
squads guarding the bejewelled patrons against ro
rioters, and the mobsters who more or less ran the city.
former Mrs McCormick attended, wearing, according to
newspaper report, 'her gorgeous diamond necklace, almost
inch wide and reaching practically to her waist'; Mrs Insu
wore pearls and 'a wide diamond bracelet.') Mankiewicz must
have placed the episode of the opera house in Chicago in
order to give it roots – to make it connect with what the public
already knew about Chicago and robber barons and opera.
(Chicago was big on opera; it was there that the infant Orson
Welles played Madame Butterfly's love child.) Insull's opera
house never really had a chance to prove or disprove his
financial theories. Mary Garden quit after one year there,
calling it 'that long black hole,' and in 1932, when Insull's
mammoth interlocking directorate of power plants collapsed
and he fled to Greece, the opera house was closed. Insull was
extradited, and in the mid-thirties he stood trial for fraud and
embezzlement; he died two years before *Citizen Kane* was
written.

The fretful banality of Susan Alexander is clearly derived
from Mankiewicz's hated old adversary Mrs Insull – notorious
for her 'discordant twitter' and her petty dissatisfaction with
everything. The Insulls had been called the least popular
couple who had ever lived in Chicago, and there was ample
evidence that they hadn't even liked each other. Opera and
the Insulls provided cover for Mankiewicz and Welles.
George J. Schaefer, who is quite open about this, says that
when he couldn't get an opening for *Kane*, because the
theatres were frightened off by the stories in the Hearst press
about injunctions and lawsuits, he went to see Hearst's
lawyers in Los Angeles and took the position that Kane could

expected to be fooled; it was simply a

..ctual (and malicious) scrap of Hearst's
..idea in the first draft. As Mankiewicz
..was to make her début in Massenet's *Thaïs*.
..ng man, Hearst had been briefly engaged to the
..sco singer Sybil Sanderson. In order to break the
..ent, Miss Sanderson's parents had sent her to study
..s, where she became well known in opera and as the
..stant companion' of Massenet, who wrote *Thaïs* for her.
..ut to use *Thaïs* would have cost a fee, so Bernard Herrmann
wrote choice excerpts of a fake French-Oriental opera –
Salammbô. (Dorothy Comingore did her own singing in the
movie except for the opera-house sequence; that was dubbed
by a professional singer who deliberately sang badly.) The
Kane amalgam may also contain a dab or two from the lives
of other magnates, such as Frank Munsey and Pulitzer, and
more than a dab from the life of Jules Brulatour, who got his
start in business by selling Eastman Kodak film. Hope
Hampton, his blond protégée and later his wife, had a career
even more ridiculous than Susan Alexander's. After she failed
as a movie actress, Brulatour financed her career at the
Chicago Opera Company at the end of the twenties, and then,
using his power to extend credit to movie companies for film
stock, he pushed the near-bankrupt Universal to star her in a
1937 disaster, in which she sang eight songs.

The only other major addition to Hearst's actual history
comes near the beginning of the movie. The latter days of
Susan Alexander as a tawdry-looking drunken singer at El
Rancho in Atlantic City, where she is billed as 'Susan
Alexander Kane' – which tells us at once that she is so poor an
entertainer that she must resort to this cheap attempt to
exploit her connection with Kane – may have been lifted from
the frayed end of Evelyn Nesbit's life. After her divorce from

Harry K. Thaw – the rich socialite who murdered Stanford White on her account – she drifted down to appearing in honky-tonks, and was periodically denounced in the press for 'capitalizing her shame.'

24

Dorothy Comingore says, 'When I read for Orson, Herman was in the room, with a broken leg and a crutch, and Orson turned to him and said, "What do you think?" And Herman said, "Yes, she looks precisely like the image of a kitten we've been looking for." '

The handling of Susan Alexander is a classic of duplicity. By diversifying the material and combining several careers, Mankiewicz could protect himself. He could claim that Susan wasn't meant to be Marion Davies – that she was nothing at all like Marion, whom he called a darling and a minx. He could point out that Marion wasn't a singer and that Hearst had never built an opera house for her – and it was true, she wasn't and he hadn't, but she was an actress and he did run Cosmopolitan Pictures for her. Right at the beginning of the movie, Kane was said to be the greatest newspaper tycoon of this or any other generation, so he was obviously Hearst; Xanadu was transparently San Simeon; and Susan's fake stardom and the role she played in Kane's life spelled Marion Davies to practically everybody in the Western world. And even though Mankiewicz *liked* Marion Davies, he was the same Mankiewicz who couldn't resist the disastrous 'Imagine – the whole world wired to Harry Cohn's ass!' He skewered her with certain identifying details that were just too good to resist, such as her love of jigsaw puzzles. They were a feature of San Simeon; the puzzles, which sometimes took two weeks to complete, were set out on tables in the salon, and the guests would work at them before lunch. And when Kane destroys Susan's room in a rage after she leaves him, he turns up a hidden bottle of booze, which was a vicious touch, coming from Mankiewicz, who had often been the beneficiary of Marion's secret cache. He provided bits that had a special *frisson* for those in the know.

One can sometimes hurt one's enemies, but that's nothing compared to what one can do to one's friends. Marion Davies, living in the style of the royal courtesans with a man who couldn't marry her without messes and scandal (his wife, Millicent, had become a Catholic, and she had also given him five sons), was an easy target. Hearst and Louella Parsons had set her up for it, and she became the victim of *Citizen Kane*. In her best roles, Marion Davies was a spunky, funny, beautiful girl, and that's apparently what she *was* and why Hearst adored her. But, in his adoration, he insisted that the Hearst press overpublicize her and overpraise her constantly, and the public in general got wise. A typical Davies film would open with the theatre ventilating system pouring attar of roses at the audience, or the theatre would be specially redecorated, sometimes featuring posters that famous popular artists had done of her in the costumes of the picture. Charity functions of which she was the queen would be splashed all over the society pages, and the movie would be reviewed under eight-column headlines. In the news section, Mayor Hylan of New York would be saying, '*When Knighthood Was in Flower* is unquestionably the greatest picture I have ever seen. ... No person can afford to miss this great screen masterpiece,' or '*Little Old New York* is unquestionably the greatest screen epic I have ever looked upon, and Marion Davies is the most versatile screen star ever cast in any part. The wide range of her stellar acting is something to marvel at. ... Every man, woman and child in New York City ought to see this splendid picture. ... I must pay my tribute to the geniuses in all lines who created such a masterpiece.'

When the toadying and praise were already sickening,

Hearst fell for one of the dumbest smart con tricks of all time: A young movie reviewer named Louella O. Parsons, working for the *New York Telegraph* for $110 a week, wrote a column saying that although Marion Davies' movies were properly publicized, the star herself wasn't publicized *enough*. Hearst fell for it and hired Parsons at $250 a week, and she began her profitable lifework of praising (and destroying) Marion Davies. Some of Davies' costume spectacles weren't bad – and she was generally charming in them – but the pictures didn't have to be bad for all the corrupt drumbeaters to turn the public's stomach. Other actresses were pushed to stardom and were accepted. (The flapper heroine Colleen Moore was Walter Howey's niece, and she was started on her career when she was fifteen. D. W. Griffith owed Howey a favour for getting *The Birth of a Nation* and *Intolerance* past the Chicago censors, and her movie contract was the payoff. She says that many of the Griffith stars were 'payoffs.') Marion Davies had more talent than most of the reigning queens, but Hearst and Louella were too ostentatious, and they never let up. There was a steady march of headlines ('Marion Davies' Greatest Film Opens Tonight'); there were too many charity balls. The public can swallow just so much: her seventy-five-thousand-dollar fourteen-room mobile 'bungalow' on the M-G-M lot, O.K.; the special carpet for alighting, no. Her pictures had to be forced on exhibitors, and Hearst spent so much on them that even when they did well, the cost frequently couldn't be recovered. One of his biographers reports a friend's saying to Hearst, 'There's money in the movies,' and Hearst's replying, 'Yes. Mine.'

Marion Davies was born in 1897, and, as a teen-ager, went right from the convent to the musical-comedy stage, where she put in two years as a dancer before Ziegfeld 'glorified' her in the 'Ziegfeld Follies of 1916.' That was where William Randolph Hearst, already in his mid-fifties, spotted her. It is said, and may even be true, that he attended the 'Follies' every night for eight weeks, buying two tickets – one for himself and the other for his hat – just 'to gaze upon her.' It is almost certainly true that from then 'to the day of his death,' as Adela Rogers St Johns put it, 'he wanted to know every minute where she was.' Marion Davies entered movies in 1917, with *Runaway Romany*, which she also wrote, and then she began that really strange, unparalleled movie career. She had starred in about fifty pictures by the time she retired, in 1937 – all under Hearst's aegis, and under his close personal supervision. (Leading men were afraid to kiss her; Hearst was always watching.) The pictures were all expensively produced, and most of them were financial failures. Marion Davies was a mimic and a parodist and a very original sort of comedienne, but though Hearst liked her to make him laugh at home, he wanted her to be a romantic maiden in the movies, and – what was irreconcilable with her talent – dignified. Like Susan, she was tutored, and he spent incredible sums on movies that would be the perfect setting for her. He appears to have been sincerely infatuated with her in old-fashioned, sentimental, ladylike roles; he loved to see her in ruffles on garden swings. But actresses didn't become public favorites in roles like those, and even if they could get by with them sometimes, they needed startling changes of pace to stay in public favor, and Hearst wouldn't let Marion Davies do anything 'sordid.'

To judge by what those who worked with her have said, she was thoroughly unpretentious, and was depressed by Hearst's taste in roles for her. She finally broke out of the costume cycle in the late twenties and did some funny pictures: *The Red Mill* (which Fatty Arbuckle, whom Hearst the moralizer had helped ruin, directed, under his new, satirical pseudonym, Will B. Goodrich), *The Fair Coed*, my childhood favorite *The Patsy*, and others. But even when she played in a slapstick parody of Gloria Swanson's career (*Show People*, in 1928),

Hearst wouldn't let her do a custard-pie sequence, despite her own pleas and those of the director, King Vidor, and the writer, Laurence Stallings. (King Vidor has described the conference that Louis B. Mayer called so that Vidor could make his case to Hearst for the plot necessity of the pie. 'Presently, the great man rose and in a high-pitched voice said, "King's right. But I'm right, too – because I'm not going to let Marion be hit in the face with a pie."') She wanted to play Sadie Thompson in *Rain,* but he wouldn't hear of it, and the role went to Gloria Swanson (and made her a star all over again). When Marion Davies should have been playing hard-boiled, good-hearted blondes, Hearst's idea of a role for her was Elizabeth Barrett Browning in *The Barretts of Wimpole Street,* and when Thalberg reserved that one for *his* lady, Norma Shearer, Hearst, in 1934, indignantly left M-G-M and took his money and his 'Cosmopolitan Pictures' label over to Warner Brothers. (The editors of his newspapers were instructed never again to mention Norma Shearer in print.) It was a long blighted career for an actress who might very well have become a big star on her own, and she finally recognized that with Hearst's help it was hopeless. By the time *Citizen Kane* came out, she had been in retirement for four years, but the sickening publicity had gone grinding on relentlessly, and, among the audiences at *Kane,* probably even those who remembered her as the charming, giddy comedienne of the late twenties no longer trusted their memories.

Mankiewicz, catering to the public, gave it the empty, stupid, no-talent blonde it wanted – the 'confidential' back-stairs view of the great gracious lady featured in the Hearst press. It was, though perhaps partly inadvertently, a much worse betrayal than if he'd made Susan more like Davies, because movie audiences assumed that Davies was a pathetic whiner like Susan Alexander, and Marion Davies was nailed to the cross of harmless stupidity and nothingness, which in high places is the worst joke of all.

25

Right from the start of movies, it was a convention that the rich were vulgarly acquisitive but were lonely and miserable and incapable of giving or receiving love. As a mass medium, movies have always soothed and consoled the public with the theme that the rich can buy everything except what counts – love. (The convention remains, having absorbed the *Dolce Vita* variation that the rich use each other sexually because they are incapable of love.) It was consistent with this popular view of the emptiness of the lives of the rich to make Susan Alexander a cartoon character; the movie reduces Hearst's love affair to an infatuation for a silly, ordinary nothing of a girl, as if everything in his life were synthetic, his passion vacuous, and the object of it a cipher. What happened in Hearst's life was far more interesting: he took a beautiful, warm-hearted girl and made her the best-known kept woman in America and the butt of an infinity of dirty jokes, and he did it out of love and the blindness of love.

Citizen Kane, however, employs the simplification, so convenient to melodrama, that there is a unity between a man's private life and his public one. This simplification has enabled ambitious bad writers to make reputations as thinkers, and in the movies of the forties it was given a superficial plausibility by popular Freudianism. Hideous character defects traceable to childhood traumas explained just about anything the authors disapproved of. Mankiewicz certainly knew better, but as a screenwriter he dealt in ideas that had popular appeal. Hearst was a notorious anti-union, pro-Nazi Red-baiter, so Kane must have a miserable, deformed childhood. He must be *wrecked* in infancy. It was a movie convention going back to silents that when you did a bio or a thesis picture you started with the principal characters as children and showed them to be miniature versions of their later characters. This convention almost invariably pleased audiences, because it also demonstrated the magic of movies – the kids so extraordinarily resembled the adult actors they would turn into. And it wasn't just makeup – they really did, having been searched out for that resemblance. (This is *possible* in theatre, but it's rarely feasible.) That rather old-fashioned view of the predestination of character from childhood needed only a small injection of popular Freudian-ism to pass for new, and if you tucked in a trauma, you took care of the motivation for the later events. Since nothing very bad had happened to Hearst, Mankiewicz drew upon Little Orson Annie. He *orphaned* Kane, and used that to explain Hearst's career. (And, as Welles directed it, there's more real emotion and pain in the childhood separation sequence than in all the rest of the movie.)

Thus Kane was emotionally stunted. Offering personal emptiness as the explanation of Hearst's career really doesn't do much but feed the complacency of those liberals who are eager to believe that conservatives are 'sick' (which is also how conservatives tend to see liberals). Liberals were willing to see this hollow-man explanation of Hearst as something much deeper than a cliché of popular melodrama, though the film's explaining his attempts to win public office and his empire-building and his art collecting by the childhood loss of maternal love is as unilluminating as the conservative conceit that Marx was a revolutionary because he hated his father. The point of the film becomes the cliché irony that although Hearst has everything materially, he has nothing humanly.

Quite by chance, I saw William Randolph Hearst once, when I was about nineteen. It was Father's Day, which sometimes falls on my birthday, and my escort bumped me into him on the dance floor. I can't remember whether it was at the Palace Hotel in San Francisco or at the St Francis, and I can't remember the year, though it was probably 1938. But I remember Hearst in almost terrifying detail, with the kind of memory I generally have only for movies. He was dinner-dancing, just like us, except that his table was a large one. He was seated with Marion Davies and his sons with their wives or dates; obviously, it was a kind of family celebration. I had read the then current *Hearst, Lord of San Simeon* and Ferdinand Lundberg's *Imperial Hearst,* and probably almost everything else that was available about him, and I remember thinking, as I watched him, of Charles A. Beard's preface to the Lundberg book – that deliberately cruel premature 'Farewell to William Randolph Hearst,' with its tone of 'He will depart loved by few and respected by none whose respect is worthy of respect. . . . None will be proud to do honor to his memory,' and so on. You don't expect to bump into a man on the dance floor after you've been reading that sort of thing about him. It was like stumbling onto Caligula, and Hearst looked like a Roman emperor mixing with the commoners on a night out. He was a huge man – six feet four or five – and he was old and heavy, and he moved slowly about the dance floor with *her.* He seemed like some prehistoric monster gliding among the couples, quietly majestic, towering over everyone; he had little, odd eyes, like a whale's, and they looked pulled down, sinking into his cheeks. Maybe I had just never seen anybody so massive and dignified and old *dancing,* and maybe it was that plus who he was, but I've never seen anyone else who seemed to incarnate power and solemnity as he did; he was frightening and he was impressive, almost as if he were wearing ceremonial robes of office. When he danced with Marion Davies, he was indifferent to everything else. They looked isolated and entranced together; this slow, huge dinosaur clung to the frowzy-looking aging blonde in what seemed to be a ritual performance. Joined together, they were as alone as the young dancing couple in the sky with diamonds in *Yellow Submarine*. Maybe they *were* that couple of a few decades later, for they had an extraordinary romance – one that lasted thirty-two years – and they certainly had the diamonds (or *had* had them). He seemed unbelievably old to me that night, when he was probably about seventy-five; they were still together when he died, in 1951, at the age of eighty-eight.

The private pattern that was devised as a correlative (and possible explanation) of Hearst's public role was false. Hearst didn't have any (recorded) early traumas. Marion Davies did have talent, and they were an extraordinarily devoted pair; far from leaving him, when he faced bankruptcy she gave him her money and jewels and real estate, and even borrowed money to enable him to keep his newspapers. He was well loved, and *still* he was a dangerous demagogue. And, despite what Charles A. Beard said and what Dos Passos said, and despite the way Mankiewicz presented him in *Citizen Kane*, and all the rest, Hearst and his consort were hardly lonely, with all those writers around, and movie stars and directors, and Shaw, and Winston Churchill, and weekend parties with Marion Davies spiking teetotaller Calvin Coolidge's fruit punch (though only with liquor that came from fruit). Even Mrs Luce came; the pictures of Hearst on the walls at Time-Life might show him as an octopus, but who could resist an invitation? Nor did Hearst lose his attraction or his friends after he lost his *big* money. After San Simeon was stripped of its silver treasures, which were sold at auction in the thirties, the regal-party weekends were finished, but he still entertained, if less lavishly, at his smaller houses. Dos Passos played the same game as *Citizen Kane* when he wrote of Hearst 'amid the relaxing adulations of screenstars, admen, screenwriters, publicitymen, columnists, millionaire editors' – suggesting that Hearst was surrounded by third-raters and sycophantic hirelings. But the lists and the photographs of Hearst's guests tell another story. He had the one great, dazzling court of the first half of the twentieth century, and the statemen and kings, the queens and duchesses at his table were as authentic as the writers and wits and great movie stars and directors. When one considers who even those screen-writers were, it's not surprising that Hearst wanted their company. Harold Ross must have wondered what drew his old friends there, for he came, too, escorted by Robert Benchley.

It is both a limitation and *in the nature of the appeal* of popular art that it constructs false, easy patterns. Like the blind-beggar-for-luck, *Kane* has a primitive appeal that is implicit in the conception. It tells the audience that fate or destiny or God or childhood trauma has already taken revenge on the wicked – that if the rich man had a good time he has suffered remorse, or, better still, that he hasn't really enjoyed himself at all. Before Mankiewicz began writing the script, he talked about what a great love story it would be – but who would buy tickets for a movie about a rich, powerful tycoon who also found true love? In popular art, riches and power destroy people, and so the secret of Kane is that he longs for the simple pleasures of his childhood before wealth tore him away from his mother – he longs for what is available to the mass audience.

26

Even when Hearst's speeches, or facsimiles of them, were used in *Kane*, their character was transformed. If one looks at his actual remarks on property and then at Mankiewicz's adaptation of them, one can see how. Hearst's remarks are tight and slightly oblique, and it takes one an instant to realize what he's saying. Mankiewicz makes them easier to grasp (and rather florid) but kills some of their almost sinister double edge by making them consciously flip. He turns them into a joke. And when Mankiewicz didn't make the speeches flip, Welles' delivery did. When you hear Kane dictate the telegram to Cuba, you don't really think for a minute that it's *acted* on. And so the movie becomes a comic strip about Hearst, without much resonance, and certainly without much tragic resonance. Hearst, who compared himself to an elephant, *looked* like a great man. I don't think he actually was great in any sense, but he was *extraordinary*, and his power and wealth, plus his enormous size, made him a phenomenally commanding presence. Mankiewicz, like Dos Passos, may have believed that Hearst fell from greatness, or (as I suspect) Mankiewicz may have liked the facile dramatic possibilities of that approach. But he couldn't carry it out. He couldn't write the character as a tragic fallen hero, because he couldn't resist making him funny. Mankiewicz had been hacking out popular comedies and melodramas for too long to write drama; one does not *dictate* tragedy to a stenotypist. He automatically, because of his own temperament and his writing habits, turned out a bitchy satirical melodrama. Inside the three hundred and twenty-five pages of his long, ambitious first draft was the crowd-pleasing material waiting to be carved out. When one reads the long version, it's obvious what must go; if I had been doing the cutting I might have cut just about the same material. *And yet* that fat to be cut away is everything that tends to make it a political and historical drama, and what is left is the private scandals of a poor little rich boy. The scandals in the long draft – some of it, set in Italy during Kane's youth, startlingly like material that came to the screen twenty years later in *La Dolce Vita* – served a purpose beyond crowd pleasing: to show what a powerful man could cover up and get away with. Yet this, of course, went out, for reasons similar to the ones that kept Kane, unlike Hearst, from winning elected office – to reassure the public that the rich *don't* get away with it.

Welles now has a lumbering grace and a gliding, whalelike motion not unlike Hearst's, but when he played the role he became stiff and crusty as the older Kane, and something went blank in the aging process – not just because the makeup was erratic and waxy (especially in the bald-headed scenes, such as the one in the picnic tent) but because the character lost his connection with business and politics and became a fancy theatrical notion, an Expressionist puppet. Also, there are times when the magic of movies fails. The camera comes so close that it can reveal too much: Kane as an old man was an actor trying to look old, and Welles had as yet only a schoolboy's perception of how age weighs one down. On a popular level, however, his limitations worked to his advantage; they tied in with the myth of the soulless rich.

The conceptions are basically *kitsch*; basically, *Kane* is popular melodrama – Freud plus scandal, a comic strip about Hearst. Yet, partly because of the resonance of what was left of the historical context, partly because of the juiciness of Welles' young talent and of the varied gifts and personalities others brought to the film, partly because of the daring of the attack on the most powerful and dangerous press lord known to that time, the picture has great richness and flair; it's *kitsch* redeemed. I would argue that this is what is remarkable about movies – that shallow conceptions in one area can be offset by elements playing against them or altering them or affecting the texture. If a movie is good, there is a general tendency to believe that everything in it was conceived and worked out according to a beautiful master plan, or that it is the result of the creative imagination of the director, but in movies things rarely happen that way – even more rarely than they do in opera or the theatre. There are so many variables; imagine how different the whole feeling of *Kane* would be if the film had been shot in a naturalistic style, or even if it had been made at M-G-M instead of at R.K.O. Extraordinary movies are the result of the 'right' people's getting together on the 'right' project at the 'right' time – in their lives and in history. I don't mean to suggest that a good movie is just a mess that happens to work (although there have been such cases) – only that a good movie is not always the result of a single artistic intelligence. It can be the result of a fortunate collaboration, of cross-fertilizing accidents. And I would argue that what redeems movies in general, what makes them so much easier to take than other arts, is that many talents in interaction in a work can produce something more enjoyable than one talent that is not of the highest. Because of the collaborative nature of most movies, masterpieces are rare, and even masterpieces may, like *Kane*, be full of flaws, but the interaction frequently results in special pleasures and surprises.

27

The director should be in control not because he is the sole creative intelligence but because only if he is in control can he liberate and utilize the talents of his co-workers, who languish (as directors do) in studio-factory productions. The best interpretation to put on it when a director says that a movie is totally his is not that he did it all himself but that he wasn't interfered with, that he made the choices and the ultimate decisions, that the whole thing isn't an unhappy compromise for which no one is responsible; not that he was the sole creator but almost the reverse – that he was free to use all the best ideas offered him.

Welles had a vitalizing, spellbinding talent; he was the man who brought out the best in others and knew how to use it. What keeps *Citizen Kane* alive is that Welles wasn't prevented (as so many directors are) from trying things out. He was young and *open*, and, as the members of that crew tell it – and they remember it very well, because it was the only time it ever happened for many of them – they could always talk to him and make suggestions, as long as they didn't make the suggestions publicly. Most big-studio movies were made in such a restrictive way that the crews were hostile and bored and the atmosphere was oppressive. The worst aspect of the factory system was that almost everyone worked beneath his capacity. Working on *Kane*, in an atmosphere of freedom, the designers and technicians came forth with ideas they'd been bottling up for years; they were all in on the creative process. Welles was so eager to try out new ideas that even the tough, hardened studio craftsmen where caught up by his spirit, just as his co-workers in the theatre and in radio had been. *Citizen Kane* is not a great work that suddenly burst out of a young prodigy's head. There are such works in the arts (though few, if any, in movies), but this is not one of them. It is a superb example of collaboration; everyone connected with it seems to have had the time of his life because he was able to contribute something.

Welles had just the right background for the sound era. He used sound not just as an inexpensive method of creating the illusion of halls and crowds but to create an American environment. He knew how to convey the way people feel about each other by the way they sound; he knew how they sounded in different rooms, in different situations. The directors who had been most imaginative in the use of sound in the early talkies were not Americans, and when they worked in America, as Ernst Lubitsch did, they didn't have the ear for American life that Welles had. And the good American movie directors in that period (men like Howard Hawks and John Ford and William Wellman) didn't have the background in theatre or – that key element – the background in radio. Hawks handled the dialogue expertly in *His Girl Friday*, but the other sounds are not much more imaginative than those in a first-rate stage production. When Welles came to Hollywood, at the age of twenty-four, his previous movie experience had not been on a professional level, but he already knew more about the dramatic possibilities of sound than most veteran directors, and the sound engineers responded to his inventiveness by giving him extraordinary new effects. At every point along the way, the studio craftsmen tried something out. Nearly all the thirty-five members of the R.K.O. special-effects department worked on *Kane*; roughly eighty per cent of the film was not merely printed but reprinted, in order to add trick effects and blend in painted sets and bits of stock footage. The view up from Susan singing on the opera stage to the stagehands high above on the catwalk, as one of them puts two fingers to his nose – which looks like a tilt (or a vertical pan) – is actually made up of three shots, the middle one a miniature. When the camera seems to pass through a rooftop skylight into the El Rancho nightclub where Susan works, the sign, the rooftop, and the skylight are miniatures, with a flash of lightning to conceal the cut to the full-scale interior. The craftsmen were so ingenious about giving Welles the effect he wanted that even now audiences aren't aware of how cheaply made *Citizen Kane* was.

In the case of the cinematographer, Gregg Toland, the contribution goes far beyond suggestions and technical solutions. I think he not only provided much of the visual style of *Citizen Kane* but was responsible for affecting the conception, and even for introducing a few elements that are not in the script. It's always a little risky to assign credit for ideas in movies; somebody is bound to turn up a film that used whatever it is – a detail, a device, a technique – earlier. The most one can hope for, generally, is to catch on to a few late links in the chain. It was clear that *Kane* had visual links to James Wong Howe's cinematography in *Transatlantic* (Howe, coincidentally, had also shot *The Power and the Glory*), but I had always been puzzled by the fact that *Kane* seemed to draw not only on the Expressionist theatrical style of Welles' stage productions but on the German Expressionist and Gothic movies of the silent period. In *Kane*, as in the German silents, depth was used like stage depth, and attention was frequently moved from one figure to another within a fixed frame by essentially the same techniques as on the stage – by the actors' moving into light or by a shift of the light to other actors (rather than by the fluid camera of a Renoir, which follows the actors, or the fragmentation and quick cutting of the early Russians). There were frames in *Kane* that seemed so close to the exaggerations in German films like *Pandora's Box* and *The Last Laugh* and *Secrets of a Soul* that I wondered what Welles was talking about when he said he had prepared for *Kane* by running John Ford's *Stagecoach* forty times. Even allowing for the hyperbole of the forty times, why should Orson Welles have studied *Stagecoach* and come up with a film that looked more like *The Cabinet of Dr Cagligari*? I wondered if there might be a link between Gregg Toland and the German tradition, though most of Toland's other films didn't suggest much German influence. When I looked up his credits as a cameraman, the name *Mad Love* rang a bell; I closed my eyes and visualized it, and there was the Gothic atmosphere, and the huge, dark rooms, with lighted figures, and Peter Lorre, bald, with a spoiled-baby face, looking astoundingly like a miniature Orson Welles.

Mad Love, made in Hollywood in 1935, was a dismal, static horror movie – an American version of a German film directed by the same man who had directed *The Cabinet of Dr Caligari*. The American remake, remarkable only for its photography, was directed by Karl Freund, who had been head cinematographer at Ufa, in Germany. He had worked with such great directors as Fritz Lang and F. W. Murnau and

G. W. Pabst, and, by his technical innovations, had helped create their styles; he had shot many of the German silent classics (*The Last Laugh, Variety, Metropolis, Tartuffe*). I recently looked at a print of *Mad Love,* and the resemblances to *Citizen Kane* are even greater than my memories of it suggested. Not only is the large room with the fireplace at Xanadu similar to Lorre's domain as a mad doctor, with similar lighting and similar placement of figures, but Kane's appearance and makeup in some sequences might be a facsimile of Lorre's. Lorre, who had come out of the German theatre and German films, played in a stylized manner that is visually imitated in *Kane.* And, amusingly, that screeching white cockatoo, which isn't in the script of *Kane* but appeared out of nowhere in the movie to provide an extra 'touch,' is a regular member of Lorre's household.

Gregg Toland was the 'hottest' photographer in Hollywood at the time he called Welles and asked to work with him; in March he had won the Academy Award for *Wuthering Heights,* and his other recent credits included *The Grapes of Wrath* and the film in which he had experimented with deep focus, *The Long Voyage Home.* He brought along his own four-man camera crew, who had recently celebrated their fifteenth year of working together. This picture was made with love; the year before his death, in 1948, Toland said that he had wanted to work with Welles because he was miserable and felt like a whore when he was on run-of-the-mill assignments, and that 'photographing *Citizen Kane* was the most exciting professional adventure of my career.' I surmise that part of the adventure was his finding a way to use and develop what the great Karl Freund had taught him.

Like the German cinematographers in the silent period, Toland took a more active role than the usual Hollywood cinematographer. For some years, whenever it was possible, he had been supervising the set construction of his films, so that he could plan the lighting. He probably responded to Welles' penchant for tales of terror and his desire for a portentous, mythic look, and since Welles didn't have enough financing for full-scale sets and was more than willing to try the unconventional, Toland suggested many of the Expressionist solutions. When a director is new to films, he is, of course, extremely dependent on his cameraman, and he is particularly so if he is also the star of the film, and is thus in front of the camera. Toland was a disciplined man, and those who worked on the set say he was a steadying influence on Welles; it is generally agreed that the two planned and discussed every shot together. With Welles, Toland was free to make suggestions that went beyond lighting techniques. Seeing Welles' facial resemblance to the tiny Lorre – even to the bulging eyes and the dimpled, sad expression – Toland probably suggested the makeup and the doll-like, jerky use of the body for Kane in his rage and as a lonely old man, and, having enjoyed the flamboyant photographic effect of the cockatoo in *Mad Love*, suggested that, too. When Toland provided Welles with the silent-picture setups that had been moribund under Karl Freund's direction, Welles used them in a childlike spirit that made them playful and witty. There's nothing static or Germanic in Welles' *direction*, and he had such unifying energy that just a couple of years ago an eminent movie critic cited the cockatoo in *Citizen Kane* as 'an unforced metaphor arising naturally out of the action.'

It's the Gothic atmosphere, partly derived from Toland's work on *Mad Love*, that inflates *Citizen Kane* and puts it in a different tradition from the newspaper comedies and the big bios of the thirties. *Citizen Kane* is, in some ways, a freak of art. Toland, although he used deep focus again later, reverted to a more conventional look for the films following *Kane*, directed by men who rejected technique 'for its own sake,' but he had passed on Freund's techniques to Welles. The dark, Gothic horror style, with looming figures, and with vast interiors that suggested castles rather than houses, formed the basis for much of Welles' later visual style. It suited Welles; it was the visual equivalent of The Shadow's voice – a gigantic echo chamber. Welles, too big for ordinary roles, too overpowering for normal characters, is stylized by nature – is by nature an Expressionist actor.

28

Two years after the release of *Citizen Kane*, when Herman Mankiewicz had become respectable – his career had taken a leap after *Kane*, and he had had several major credits later in 1941 and had just won another Academy nomination, for his work on *Pride of the Yankees* – he stumbled right into Hearst's waiting arms. He managed to have an accident that involved so many of the elements of his life that it sounds like a made-up surreal joke. Though some of his other calamities are lost in an alcoholic fog – people remember only the bandages and Mankiewicz's stories about how he got them, and maybe even he didn't always know the facts – this one is all too well documented.

Driving home after a few drinks at Romanoff's, he was only a block and a half from his house when he hit a tiny car right at the gates of the Marion Davies residence. And it wasn't just any little car he hit; it was one driven by Lee Gershwin – Ira Gershwin's wife, Lenore, a woman Mankiewicz had known for years. He had adapted the Gershwins' musical *Girl Crazy* to the screen in 1932, and he had known the Gershwins before that, in the twenties, in New York; they were part of the same group. It was a gruesomely comic accident: Hearst was living on the grounds of the Marion Davies estate at the time, in that bungalow that Marion had used at M-G-M and then at Warners, and he was conferring with the publisher of his *New York Journal-American* when he heard the crash. Hearst sent the publisher down to investigate, and as soon as the man reported who was involved, Hearst went into action. Lee Gershwin had had two passengers – her secretary, who wasn't hurt, and her laundress, whom she was taking home, and who just got a bump. Mrs Gershwin herself wasn't badly hurt, though she had a head injury that required some stiches. It was a minor accident, but Mankiewicz was taken to the police station, and he apparently behaved noisily and badly there. When he got home, a few hours later, his wife, Sara, sobered him up, and, having ascertained that Lee Gershwin had been treated at the hospital and had already been discharged, she sent him over to the Gershwins' with a couple of dozen roses. Marc Connelly, who was at the Gershwins' that night, says that when Mankiewicz arrived the house was full of reporters, and Ira Gershwin was serving them drinks and trying to keep things affable. Mankiewicz went upstairs to see Lee, who was lying in bed with her head bandaged. Amiable madman that he was, he noticed a painting on the bedroom wall, and his first remark was that he had a picture by the same artist. He apparently didn't have any idea that he was in serious trouble.

Hearst's persistent vindictiveness was one of his least attractive traits. Mankiewicz was charged with a felony, and the minor accident became a major front-page story in the Hearst papers across the country for four successive days, with headlines more appropriate to a declaration of war. It became the excuse for another Hearst campaign against the orgies and dissolute lives of the movie colony, and Hearst dragged it on for months. By then, the Hearst press was on its way to becoming the crank press, and Hearst had so many enemies that Mankiewicz had many friends. When Mankiewicz appealed to the American Civil Liberties Union, there had already been stories in *Time, Newsweek, Variety*, and elsewhere pointing out that the persecution in the Hearst papers was a reprisal for his having written the script of *Citizen Kane*. Mankiewicz, however, had to stand trial on a felony charge. And although he got through the mess of the trial all right, the hounding by the Hearst papers took its toll, and his reputation was permanently damaged.

In a letter to Harold Ross after the trial, Mankiewicz asked to write a Profile of Hearst that Ross was considering. 'Honestly,' he wrote, 'I know more about Hearst than any other man alive. (There are a couple of deaders before their time who knew more, I think.) I studied his career like a scholar before I wrote *Citizen Kane*.' And then, in a paragraph that suggests his admiration, despite everything, for both Hearst and Welles, he wrote, 'Shortly after I had been dragged from the obscurity of the police blotter and – a middle-aged, flat-footed, stylish-stout scenario writer – been promoted by the International News Service into Cary Grant, who, with a tank, had just drunkenly ploughed into a baby carriage occupied by the Dionne quintuplets, the Duchess of Kent, Mrs Franklin D. Roosevelt (the President's wife), and the favorite niece of the Pope, with retouched art combining the more unflattering features of Goering and Dillinger, I happened to be discussing Our Hero with Orson. With the fair-mindedness that I have always recognized as my outstanding trait, I said to Orson that, despite this and that, Mr Hearst was, in many ways, a great man. He was, and is, said Orson, a horse's ass, no more nor less, who has been wrong, without exception, on everything he's ever touched. For instance, for fifty years, said Orson, Hearst did nothing but scream about the Yellow Peril, and then he gave up his seat and hopped off two months before Pearl Harbor.'

29

In 1947, Ferdinand Lundberg sued Orson Welles, Herman J. Mankiewicz, and R.K.O. Radio Pictures, Inc., for two hundred and fifty thousand dollars for copyright infringement, charging that *Citizen Kane* had plagiarized his book *Imperial Hearst*. On the face of it, the suit looked ridiculous. No doubt (as Houseman admits) Mankiewicz had drawn upon everything available about Hearst, in addition to his own knowledge, and no doubt the Lundberg book, which brought a great deal of Hearst material together and printed some things that had not been printed before, was especially useful, but John Dos Passos might have sued on similar grounds, since material that was in *U.S.A.* was also in the movie, and so might dozens of magazine writers. Hearst himself might have sued, on the basis that he hadn't been credited with the dialogue. The defense would obviously be that the material was in the public domain, and the suit looked like the usual nuisance-value suit that Hollywood is plagued by – especially since Lundberg offered to settle for a flat payment of $18,000. But R.K.O. had become one of Howard Hughes' toys in the late forties, and a crew of expensive lawyers was hired. When the suit came to trial, in 1950, Welles was out of the country; he had given his testimony earlier, in the form of a deposition taken before the American vice-consul at Casablanca, Morocco. This deposition is a curious document, full of pontification and evasion and some bluffing so outrageous that one wonders whether the legal stenographer was able to keep a straight face. *Citizen Kane* had already begun to take over and change the public image of Hearst; Hearst and Kane had become inseparable, as Welles and Kane were, but Welles possibly didn't really know in detail – or, more likely, simply didn't remember – how close the movie was to Hearst's life. He seemed more concerned with continuing the old pretense that the movie was not about Hearst than with refuting

Lundberg's charge of plagiarism, and his attempts to explain specific incidents in the movie as if their relationship to Hearst were a mere coincidence are fairly funny. He stated that 'I have done no research into the life of William Randolph Hearst at any time,' and that 'in writing the screenplay of *Citizen Kane* I drew entirely upon my own observations of life,' and then was helpless to explain how there were so many episodes from Hearst's life in the movie. When he was cornered with specific details, such as the picture of Jim Gettys in prison clothes, he gave up and said, 'The dialogue for the scene in question was written in its first and second draftings exclusively by my colleague Mr Mankiewicz. I worked on the third draft.' When he was read a long list of events in the film that parallel Hearst's life as it is recorded in *Imperial Hearst*, he tried to use the Insull cover story and came up with the surprising information that the film dealt 'quite as fully with the world of grand opera as with the world of newspaper publishing.'

Mankiewicz, in a preparatory statement, freely admitted that many of the incidents and details came from Hearst's life but said that he knew them from personal acquaintance and from a lifetime of reading. He was called to testify at the trial, and John Houseman was called as a witness to Mankiewicz's labor on the script. Mankiewicz was indignant that anyone could suggest that a man of his knowledge would need to crib, and he paraded his credentials. It was pointed out that John Gunther had said Mankiewicz made better sense than all the politicians and diplomats put together, and that he was widely known to have a passionate interest in contemporary history, particularly as it related to power, and to have an enormous library. And, of course, he had known Hearst in the years of his full imperial glory, and his friends knew of his absorption in everything to do with Hearst. According to Houseman, he and Mankiewicz thought they were both brilliant in court;

they treated the whole suit as an insult, and enjoyed themselves so much while testifying that they spent the time between appearances on the stand congratulating each other. Mankiewicz, in a final gesture of contempt for the charge, brought an inventory of his library and tossed it to the R.K.O. lawyers to demonstrate the width and depth of his culture. It was an inventory that Sara had prepared some years before, when (during a stretch of hard times) they had rented out their house on Tower Road; no one had bothered to look at the inventory – not even the R.K.O. attorneys before they put it into evidence. But Lundberg's lawyers did; they turned to 'L,' and there, neatly listed under 'Lundberg,' were three copies of *Imperial Hearst*. During Mankiewicz's long recuperation, his friends had sent him many books, and since his friends knew of his admiration for many sides of the man he called 'the outstanding whirling pagoda of our times,' he had been showered with copies of this particular book. The inventory apparently made quite an impression in court, and the tide turned. The jury had been cordial to Mankiewicz's explanation of how it was that he knew details that were in the Lundberg book and were unpublished elsewhere, but now the width and depth of his culture became suspect. After thirty days, the trial resulted in a hung jury, and rather than go through another trial, R.K.O. settled for $15,000 – and also paid an estimated couple of hundred thousand dollars in lawyers' fees and court costs.

Mankiewicz went on writing scripts, but his work in the middle and late forties is not in the same spirit as *Kane*. It's rather embarrassing to look at his later credits, because they are yea-saying movies – decrepit 'family pictures' like *The Enchanted Cottage*. The booze and the accidents finally added up, and he declined into the forties sentimental slop. He tried to rise above it. He wrote the script he had proposed earlier on Aimee Semple McPherson, and he started the one on

Dillinger, but he had squandered his health as well as his talents. I have read the McPherson script; it is called *Woman of the Rock*, and it's a tired, persevering-to-the-end, burned-out script. He uses a bit of newspaper atmosphere, and Jed again, this time as a reporter, and relies on a flashback structure from Aimee's death to her childhood; there are 'modern' touches – a semi-lesbian lady who manages the evangelist, for instance – and the script comes to life whenever he introduces sophisticated characters, but he can't write simple people, and even the central character is out of his best range. The one device that is interesting is the heroine's love of bright scarves, starting in childhood with one her father gives her and ending with one that strangles her when it catches on a car wheel, but this is stolen from Isadora Duncan's death, and to give the death of one world-famous lady to another is depressingly poverty-stricken. Mankiewicz's character hadn't changed. He had written friends that he bore the scars of his mistake with Charlie Lederer, but just as he had lent the script of *Kane* to Lederer, Marion Davies' nephew, he proudly showed *Woman of the Rock* to Aimee Semple McPherson's daughter, Roberta Semple, and that ended the project. His behavior probably wasn't deliberately self-destructive as much as it was a form of innocence inside the worldly, cynical man – I visualize him as so *pleased* with what he was doing that he wanted to share his delight with others. I haven't read the unfinished Dillinger; the title, *As the Twig Is Bent*, tells too hoary much.

In his drama column in *The New Yorker* in 1925, Mankiewicz parodied those who thought the Marx Brothers had invented all their own material in *The Cocoanuts* and who failed to recognize George S. Kaufman's contribution. It has been Mankiewicz's fate to be totally ignored in the books on the Marx Brothers movies; though his name is large in the original ads, and though Groucho Marx and Harry Ruby and

S. J. Perelman all confirm the fact that he functioned as the producer of *Monkey Business* and *Horse Feathers*, the last reference I can find to this in print is in *Who's Who in America* for 1953, the year of his death. Many of the thirties movies he wrote are popular on television and at college showings, but when they have been discussed in film books his name has never, to my knowledge appeared. He is never mentioned in connection with *Duck Soup*, though Groucho confirms the fact that he worked on it. He is now all but ignored even in many accounts of *Citizen Kane*. By the fifties, his brother Joe – with *A Letter to Three Wives* and *All About Eve* – had become the famous wit in Hollywood, and there wasn't room for two Mankiewiczes in movie history; Herman became a parenthesis in the listings for Joe.

30

Welles has offered his semi-defiant apologia for his own notoriously self-destructive conduct in the form of the old fable that he tells as Arkadin in *Confidential Report*, of 1955 – an 'original screenplay' that, from internal evidence, he may very well have written. A scorpion wants to get across a lake and asks a frog to carry him on his back. The frog obliges, but midway the scorpion stings him. As they both sink, the frog asks the scorpion why he did it, pointing out that now he, too, will die, and the scorpion answers, 'I know, but I can't help it; it's my character.' The fable is inserted conspicuously, as a personal statement, almost as if it were a confession, and it's a bad story for a man to use as a parable of his life, since it's a disclaimer of responsibility. It's as if Welles believed in predestination and were saying that he was helpless. Yet Welles' characterization of himself seems rather odd. Whom, after all, has he fatally stung? He was the catalyst for the only moments of triumph that most of his associates ever achieved.

Every time someone in the theatre or in movies breaks

through and does something good, people expect the moon of him and hold it against him personally when he doesn't deliver it. That windy speech Kaufman and Hart gave their hero in *The Fabulous Invalid* indicates the enormous burden of people's hopes that Welles carried. He has a long history of disappointing people. In the *Saturday Evening Post* of January 20, 1940, Alva Johnston and Fred Smith wrote:

> Orson was an old war horse in the infant prodigy line by the time he was ten. He had already seen eight years' service as a child genius. . . . Some of the oldest acquaintances of Welles have been disappointed in his career. They see the twenty-four-year-old boy of today as a mere shadow of the two-year-old man they used to know.

A decade after *Citizen Kane*, the gibes were no longer so good-natured; the terms 'wonder boy' and 'boy genius' were thrown in Welles' face. When Welles was only thirty-six, the normally gracious Walter Kerr referred to him as 'an international joke, and possibly the youngest living has-been.' Welles had the special problems of fame without commercial success. Because of the moderate financial returns on *Kane*, he lost the freedom to control his own productions; after *Kane*, he never had complete control of a movie in America. And he lost the collaborative partnerships that he needed. For whatever reasons, neither Mankiewicz nor Houseman nor Toland ever worked on another Welles movie. He had been advertised as a one-man show; it was not altogether his own fault when he became one. He was alone, trying to be 'Orson Welles,' though 'Orson Welles' had stood for the activities of a group. But he needed the family to hold him together on a project and to take over for him when his energies became scattered. With them, he was a prodigy of accomplishments; without them, he flew apart, became disorderly. Welles lost his magic touch, and as his films began to be diffuse he acquired the reputation of being an intellectual, difficult-to-understand artist. When he appears on television to recite from Shakespeare or the Bible, he is introduced as if he were the epitome of the highbrow; it's television's more polite way of cutting off his necktie.

The Mercury players had scored their separate successes in *Kane*, and they went on to conventional careers; they had hoped to revolutionize theatre and films, and they became part of the industry. Turn on the TV and there they are, dispersed, each in old movies or his new series or his reruns. Away from Welles and each other, they were neither revolutionaries nor great originals, and so Welles became a scapegoat – the man who 'let everyone down.' He has lived all his life in a cloud of failure because he hasn't lived up to what was unrealistically expected of him. No one has ever been able to do what was expected of Welles – to create a new radical theatre and to make one movie masterpiece after another – but Welles' 'figurehead' publicity had snowballed to the point where all his actual and considerable achievements looked puny compared to what his destiny was supposed to be. In a less confused world, his glory would be greater than his guilt.